# sex and the church girl

*how the church has formed, informed,
and sometimes misinformed the sexuality of women*

# sex and the church girl

*how the church has formed, informed, and sometimes misinformed the sexuality of women*

Edited by Tracey M. Lewis-Giggetts

BOOKS AND MEDIA

SEX AND THE CHURCH GIRL

*How the Church Has Formed, Informed, and Sometimes Misinformed the Sexuality of Women*

© 2019 by NewSeason Books and Media, LLC

NewSeason Books and Media, LLC
PO Box 1403
Havertown, PA 19083
www.nsbooksandmedia.com

ISBN: 978-1-7336472-0-5

*How Not to Lose Your Virginity* and *The Surprise of the Angry Virgins* will appear in the forthcoming book, *Ragamuffin Diva: A Memoir in Essays* by Claudia Love Mair.

All rights reserved. No part of this book may be reproduced in any form or by any means including electronic, mechanical or photocopying or stored in a retrieval system without permission in writing from the publisher except by a reviewer who may quote brief passages to be included in a review.

## contents

**from the editor**
i

**1 how not to lose your virginity**  claudia love mair
1

**2 the surprise of the angry virgins (part two)**  claudia love mair
9

**3 defining myself, for myself**  felecia commodore
17

**4 pearls for my mother**  jessica "souletic" harris
31

**5 open legs didn't heal my empty heart**  angela johnson ayers
39

**6 the bible is not a sex manual (and other uncomfortable truths)**
alexus rhone
49

**7 body versus**..leah williams-tate
61

**8 warm and fuzzies**  cyndi swinton-jackson
69

**9 taming a cockscomb**  sharon d. moore
79

**10 left to my own vices**  rainah chambliss
95

**11 what they didn't teach me in sunday school**  candace e. wilkins
105

**meet the writers**
113

# from the editor

I think about death every day. I regularly imagine my own demise or the demise of those I love in the most horrific of ways. These aren't suicidal ideations in the sense that I never envision my death as coming from my own hand. Nevertheless, for now, I can't make these imaginings stop. I want to. I go to therapy twice a month to gain the tools to be able to counter these thoughts with ones that are more life-giving but, for now, they are a part of my life.

I consider this aspect of my thought life as, ironically, a kind of Paulian thorn in the side. These thoughts certainly have weight. They matter in that they can cause anything from a brief hesitation in decision making to a full-on panic attack. But I refuse to let them stop me from moving forward. From pursuing my purpose. From living out my dreams.

I'm also acutely aware that my mind's preoccupation with death is rooted in fear. Fear of being out of control. Fear of evils known and unknown. This is the gift given to me by PTSD (Post-Traumatic Stress Disorder). It is the way my mind chooses to cope with anything that feels unstable. It is the how my body first learned to respond to the sexual trauma I experienced as a child and young adult.

I wish I could say that being a member of various churches over the years has facilitated my healing process. I think I've stopped hoping for that. I know that my faith in Jesus has certainly held me together when I thought anxiety and PTSD would take me out, but as far as having a community of people to support my truth, a place where I can be freely myself and all the baggage that comes with that—well, that hasn't been my experience. In fact, in order to maintain my faith at all, I have to separate my relationship with Jesus from my relationship with the Church. It is in the church where I learned how to play the game, smile and stand on cue, and pretend like my life is picture perfect. If I'm honest, it is church folks who are the ones most "concerned" by me putting this book together. Church is the place where I learned that it's better to hide my story than tell it.

I'm aware of what many people in the church—sometimes even women who themselves are survivors—believe about people like me. Their go-to thought is that a person "asked for it" somehow. Even if that person is a child. Even if they are a woman of faith. Their first instinct is to protect men. To protect leadership. "Touch not God's Anointed," they say while never discerning whether the person they are protecting is actually God's anointed in the first place. And, of course, everything changes when you start talking about it. Even as I read and edited the stories in this book, some filled with positive or neutral experiences, others not so much, I found myself thinking about the ways in which our faith traditions are complicit in some of the traumatic experiences women face either in the church or when we try to turn to the church for help.

There are a myriad of memories associated with my sexual trauma. Molestation as a child brought on a kind of deep, under the marrow, fear that has always been hard to explain. Being raped at the age of 23 intensified that fear and made future relationships challenging to navigate. The most consistent part of either situation is that I could never go to the church for any kind of facilitation of my healing. At my most well, I certainly tried. But I learned quickly that I could never count on the church for that.

When I returned to my home after being sent away for over a year to live with other family members after my abuse, no one talked to me about it. I wasn't sent to therapy. I'm not sure anyone even considered what that experience might have done to me mentally and emotionally. In hindsight, I recognize that the people in my life were not equipped to do that kind of healing work for themselves much less help me do it. But as a child, I had questions. I had pain. I had curiosities. And no one helped me sort through those questions or pain. No one helped me explore my curiosities in healthy ways. The mentality of those around me was "move on."

*Moving on* in my childhood looked like lots of church. My parents "got saved" not too long after I returned home, and my world became fully immersed in church life. Youth choirs and bible conferences. Sunday school and bible drill teams. Some of these were a great foundation for the faith I embrace today. Some of it, much of it, felt false. It felt like a mask I was being forced to wear. A mask that would hide the complexities of my life story up until that point. Nobody ever actually said it, but the message was clear: Don't talk about what happened. Do not air our dirty laundry. No, it doesn't matter how much it hurts you on the inside. On the outside, shut your mouth and memorize your verses.

And I obeyed. I obeyed to the detriment of my own spiritual and emotional development. I obeyed because I somehow believed that's what Jesus wanted. That proverbial mask eventually became a nearly permanent fixture on my soul.

I wouldn't remove it until I was almost 40.

So that's why I compiled these essays. I wanted to do this book because these women's stories are not uncommon. I wanted to do this because I know there are so many women of faith who are wearing their own masks. Maybe it's not the result of sexual trauma. Maybe it's misinformation about the nature of sex and sexuality. Maybe it's the confusion on what the Bible actually says about sex. Maybe it's a constant reckoning with the desire to live up to whatever unreasonable expectations were set for us as young girls.

Even as a child, I knew deep down that I wasn't getting the whole story from the churches of my youth and early adulthood. I knew deep down underneath the machinations and manipulations of various church doctrines that God didn't want me to live with such a heavy weight. I've finally laid down that weight. And my prayer is that you will, too. Yes, I suppose that is the goal in publishing this collection. We don't have to be afraid of talking about sex. We don't have to be afraid to share our personal sexual journeys. We can lay down the weights we've been given. We can be free.

> Tracey M. Lewis-Giggetts
> Founder and Chief Creative Officer
> NewSeason Books and Media

# 1

# how not to lose your virginity

## claudia love mair

*"I charge you, daughters of Jerusalem,
by all gazelles and wild does, do not rouse,
do not wake my beloved before she pleases."*
                              -Song of Solomon 2:7

1. Make sure it's summer and hot enough to track heatwaves in the air outside. It helps if inside of you an inferno burns, one that is no holy fire.

2. Don't let your mother know you're what she would call "hot to trot." Otherwise, she will be sure to keep you relatively safe.

3. Write letters to the hot boy, the beautiful one who got away. Because he's three years older than you and as gorgeous as the sun, wait until he's a grown ass man before you do this. After some stalking, find out he is in the Navy, and send him adoring missives.

4. Swoon when he writes you back, your swollen little heart hardly capable of taking it all in. Say, "Glory be, he's come to Jesus," when you find out he's a Christian, too. Write each other in glowing terms about spiritual things. Well, mostly spiritual things.

5. Love him with outrageous passion, the striking boy who will soon become a model. Enjoy when he writes back saying all the right things, no matter how improbable it is that a man like him will ever be into you. Buy it all, every bullshit thing he says. Cash out on his sweet talk.

6. It's important to think you're a grown ass woman, even though it will be months before you're old enough to vote. Tell him you aren't like you were the first time you met, a wide-eyed child of fourteen, wearing sweat socks folded down for bobby socks in your thick soled Mary Janes, devastated by a surprised kiss from the boy who looks as good as ripe, sun warmed apples and the love of Jesus. Say you've come a looong way, drawing out the word like you're Bobby DeBarge before he starts singing, "I Call Your Name." You will sound silly and unconvincing, but try anyway.

7. Think because you had one serious boyfriend, engaged in heavy petting, and gave him a blow job that you are a veritable expert on sex, even though *technically* you're still a virgin. That technicality is significant, but you won't know it.

8. Don't tell him you've never had intercourse, and be clueless about whether or not he's clear on this fact. He will totally know you're a virgin because you act like the kid you are, but since you're only seventeen and think you're grown, you'll be the last to know how young and dumb you are.

9. Believe, bless your heart, that you don't have to worry too much about all of this sex stuff, and assume that because you're both Christians, you'll be abstinent. Mostly. In fact, be sure you won't go further than you did with that first serious boyfriend, if you even go *that* far since that first boyfriend left you for God, and wow, did that sting. No, determine that you and Gorgeous Soon to be Model will not have sex, and that settles it. Christians don't actually go all the way before marriage anyway. This ensures a blissful wedding night.

10. Have no insight to the fact that some, nay *many* single Christians have sex before marriage. They go *all* the way. Don't truly get that this is a thing because people lie like the cat on the counter top, even though you've run the damn animal off of there a thousand times.

11. Plan to meet him when he comes home on leave. Ask him in your last letter how the two of you will handle temptation because you've been reading Josh McDowell and think you've got this chastity thing on lock now. Think you know exactly what to do to stay (mostly) pure. When he sends back another sweet letter, never responding to your question, assume he

thinks it's something you should talk about face to face, even though your heart knows this is horse dookey.

12. Travel on a Greyhound bus over 250 miles to visit him when he's back home. He won't bother to see you right away, but don't let this deter you. It will take two days to catch up with him. One lonely day, after you've called and called, hold the phone against your ear and let it ring. For hours. Be that desperate.

13. When you finally speak with him on the phone, relish how funny and engaging he is, and notice he is also an asshole. He will make his position clear on this call: have sex with him, or he'll find someone else who will. His boldness will shock you. If he were to say this to you when, let's say you're fifty-four and writing your spiritual memoir, your response would surely be, "Have it with someone else, you dick." But your young, obsessed heart is kind of breaking, so tell him you *will* have sex with him.

14. Don't mention that you're scared, or that when things became hot and heavy between you and First Serious Boyfriend, and he tried to enter you, your body created its own chastity belt, and he never got inside to get the goods. Wonder if you can't really *do* sex? By all means do not tell him that all your bragging about being a grown woman is just talk, or say despite your mistakes, and that time you gave someone head, you really don't want to do something that's a sin. First Boyfriend hurt you badly when he

left you for God, as if you were the problem. You don't want to hurt like that again.

15. Avoid telling him that you try to be good, even though you fail too often. Don't, I repeat, don't tell him it means something to you to do the right thing.

16. Barely sleep the night before. God will trouble your dreams like the waters black folks wade in. In sleep, God will plead with you not to have sex with the incredible looking asshat who is already manipulating you. God will have never so furiously stalked your dreams before. He will never do it again.

17. Convince yourself that this matter is important to God, a pivotal decision for you that could change the course of your life. Be sure having sex with him is the one thing that could change *everything*. You will have no fucking clue exactly how much will change. Pun intended.

18. In the morning, devise a plan you won't know is stupid: decide you will act like you're going to do the deed, then at the last minute start to cry. Think this has a chance in hell of working, as if crying can get you out of anything.

19. When he finally shows up, forget the fact that Gorgeous Soon to be Model blew you off for two days. Wear your cutest outfit, a brand new, white prairie skirt and red western shirt, the height of fashion that season according to *Seventeen* magazine.

20. He will be all charm and unearthly good looks, in dark slacks and a light button down. Oh, how you will believe you're deeply in love. Laugh at his jokes, and gaze dreamily at him at all times. When the heat of the July day beckons country girl you to abandon your shoes, he will snap, "Put your shoes on. Don't you have any class?"

You don't, but that is beside the point. Your lack of pretension is one of coolest things about you. You love the feel of the warm ground beneath your bare feet. At home, you never think about class when you kick off your flip flops to feel the heat of the sun baked pavement. But let his judgey question go because he is the prettiest man you've ever seen, and holy mackerel, you will never, ever get another one that looks like him. In fact, be sure another man as fine as him doesn't exist. You will be wrong about this, so ridiculously in love. Or thinking you're in love.

Or maybe you're obsessed.

Whatever.


21. When he offers you the option of going to a motel, say no because the thought of doing that makes you feel promiscuous with a plan. So willingly let him take you to one of the empty brownstones his parents have not yet rented out. A dusty mattress will lie in the middle of the floor, with a yellow blanket flung over it. Realize you should have chosen the damn motel.

22. The boy will take your hand and pull you over and onto the mattress. He will take you into his strong arms. When it's time for the fake tears to start, you will instead revel in how good he feels, how right. He will smell like the Stetson cologne you gave him because you do not yet have taste. He will kiss your neck and nibble your ear, and you will not feel like crying at all. You'll come alive when he presses his lips to your hot skin, and flush pink with pleasure. You are going to want more of him, more than you've ever wanted anything. The God dreams will be banished from memory. Oh, Lordy, you will feel starved for his touch, and when he lays you back, you'll willingly go down.

23. It will be over very soon. You won't be able to tolerate the sharp, unbearable pain of it. You will beg him to stop, and to his credit, he will immediately. That will be the only gentlemanly thing he does from then on.

"Go home and tell you little friends you tried to do it," he will say, shattering your dignity.

You will not know you can say, "Fuck you."

When you were a child, you had an illustrated book of Bible stories, the one advertised in every pediatrician's office in America in the seventies. In the chapter where Adam and Eve are banished from the garden, Eve is pictured amid ominous clouds, her hands raised to protect her head as if God is about to knock the hell out of her. As you lie there steeped in shame, you will understand how Eve must have felt. You will feel banished from God's presence and realize the pretty boy wasn't worth it.

But you will reply to his harsh words with a tiny, barely audible, "Oh." The little "oh" that says, "God, I am so, so sorry I did this to you."

It will be many years later before you realize you are sorry you did this to yourself.

# 2

# the surprise of the angry virgins (part two)

## claudia love mair

True love waits, but I didn't. He was beautiful, a rare specimen of male so devastatingly fine the odds were against me at first glance. I surrendered my virginity to him on a dusty mattress in a furniture-less house his parents used as a rental property. When he was done thirty seconds later at my insistence, he told me to go home and tell my little friends I tried to do it. Nope. Definitely not true love.

By the time True Love Waits was an international Christian abstinence group, then movement, and purity was a culture, it was the nineties, and I was thirty-ish, but I took the pledge:

*Believing that true love waits, I make a commitment to God, myself, my family, my friends, my future mate and my future children to be sexually abstinent from this day until the day I enter a biblical marriage relationship.*

Hashtag Claudia Fail. Repeatedly, and more often than not, with great pleasure. But there were tribulations. Men who refused to respect me. Pregnancies that failed. Pregnancies that didn't. I wore shame like it was the only outfit I owned, a cheap, ill-fitting dress from Dots. I couldn't change my past, but maybe I could teach my children and Godchildren, boys and girls, to do better. So I set out to raise *True Love Waits* kids in a postmodern, sex-saturated world.

I started with the girls. I was sure they were more vulnerable. Then, I proceeded with the same lessons for the boys. Then the Godbabies. I told them *true loves wait*. That sex is personal. I told them that they needed to trust the person they were with because they would literally, and figuratively, be naked with them. I told them to wait for the guy or gal who was crazy about them and loved them enough to spend their life with them. I never wanted my babies to experience a funky mattress in an empty house and a person who would humiliate them, rather than honor them right after.

Did you notice something about that last sentence? It was about me. It was *all* about me. What I taught my children in those tender years came filtered through the lens of my shame.

I did not celebrate their bodies, their feelings, or their sacred sexuality. I was too busy focusing on protecting them from failures that were wholly mine. I meant well, but that doesn't mean I did well.

As my daughters and sons, biological and spiritual, grew older, they mostly ignored my admonitions. I witnessed their awareness of sex bud like breasts, hips, facial hair, and men's voices. I knew some of my kids didn't know if they would wait for marriage. And some of my Godbabies were already sexually active when they came into my life. They chose to stay that way. The knowledge that I had failed to convince them to wait for sex made me take to the bed, weeping all night and feeling like I was God's biggest disappointment.

Do you see what I did there? Made it about me again. This was a recurring theme in my parenting. While I worked hard to nag holiness into my children, I forgot to dialogue with them about what *they* wanted, what they longed for.

I had this conversation with one of my girls. Whether she's daughter or Goddaughter, I can't say. She asked me not to. The whole matter embarrasses her.

My beloved girl: "You've been telling me to stay a virgin since I was a kid, and now I don't know how to deal with men. I don't even feel comfortable kissing. How am I supposed to be normal? No guy is going to want to take his time and teach me."

Me: "If he loves you, he will."

But the truth is, I'm not convinced. Life moves at a much faster pace for millennials and gen-Zers than it did for me. The blessed assurance I want to give all my loves is built on faith, not facts. I *believe* she'll find a good man who will wait for her. I didn't find that, but of course, I think it's right to saddle all the young people in my life with ideals I never lived up to. I even passed these aspirations on to my fiction readers. I thought it was what God wanted of me, a sort of penance for my own sins.

A few years later, my sweet beloved, older now, feels even worse. Her friends have learned who they are as sexual beings, what works for them, and what doesn't. These young women are comfortable asking for and receiving what they need in bed, while my angry virgin, as beautiful as she is, hasn't been on a proper date. She constantly fields the question, "Have you *been* with anybody yet?" People's implication that she is a unicorn has become increasingly clear to her. She, however, does not wish to be rare. She wants to be a regular person, with normal, healthy ideas about sex.

I think about my own sex education and picture myself at thirteen, seated at the big, metal 1950s kitchen table in the house where I grew up. Mama is across from me, tired as usual, a loose house dress sagging on her shoulders.

"Keep your dress down and your panties up," she says. She watches my appalled face while issuing this succinct exhortation, but my embarrassment doesn't move her. She's already had a daughter sixteen and pregnant by an older man. She is not here for any foolishness from me. I'm afraid to ask questions. I can tell by her demeanor the conversation is over.

Mother Church said, "Wait on the Lord. You will be blessed." This edict over and over, in church, at marriage seminars I went to, even though I wasn't married, and in the fierce, protective cloud of hovering church mothers, the kind who eyed the length of my skirt, and had no qualms about pulling my narrow tail to the side to get me right.

I believed them. And I believed that my failure to remain abstinent doomed me. But later, I met people who did everything right: stayed virgins, earned good grades, worked hard, and served the needy. The promised, good Christian husband never materialized for them. A perfect sex life didn't show up like a gift from above on their wedding night. Disappointed, some of them gave up God. Two of these virgins-at-marriage couples are now divorced, including the pair that didn't so much as kiss before the wedding. She divorced him because he sexually abused her. Perhaps she would have known his proclivities if they'd had sex previously. Just saying. The woman from the other divorced couple spiraled into sometimes out of control sex with at least one emotionally abusive man. While married, she believed she didn't like sex. Now she believes she never had the right partner. These angry virgins came as a complete surprise to me. Purity was supposed to work. It was promised. "A promise is a promise," it was said to me.

By contrast, some people I know *didn't* wait on for true love, but went on to have healthy enjoyable sex lives and long-lasting relationships. How could this be? Maybe for the same reasons that the Shulamite in Song of Solomon and her beloved, two people who the scriptures do not say were married, enjoyed all kinds of great sex. They celebrated the act *shamelessly*. The Shulamite woman even had the daughters of Israel cheering her on like a private chorus. Read it and see.

I recently did a study on Biblical sex. It was enlightening, soul shattering, and often deeply affirming. There is bad sex in the Bible, and good sex, and terrible assaults, and outrageous examples of sexism. There are men God called his friends who had more than enough wives to bed down a different woman every day and still have wives to take care of. And that's just the wives. Don't get me started on the concubines. God help us all if I go in on what a godly man was permitted to do to a slave, including man to boy sex. Sanctioned by Mr. Flee Fornication, the Apostle Paul himself. This study was enough to make me cancel God, if I didn't know that the bible itself is not God. Biblical sex standards have caused a lot of young ladies I know to ditch what they view as a patriarchal book that refuses to hold men to the same standards as women, or at least view the Bible with reasonable skepticism.

In truth, sex in the Bible is as varied as the people having it. It's messy and human. By the end of my study, I truly felt like God has always had bigger things to worry about than who's zoom-a-zoom zooming whom. That's not to say sex should be casual. I don't have the heart for casual sex myself. What I mean is sex doesn't have to be a casualty of the purity movement, which numerous studies have proven did not work out for everyone who embraced it.

My talks with my beloveds are different now. I still encourage them to wait for love, but if they don't, at the very least to wait for respect. Their sexuality is all their own, however, and for better or worse, I affirm it.

"Be wise, my love," I say now. "Make sure your heart is in it."

I hope that even this doesn't heap shame on their heads.

I realize, regrettably, that I hurt my children, Godchildren, and possibly readers with my views, espousing a system that writer Christine Garter asserts, in her book, *Making Chastity Sexy: The Rhetoric of Evangelical Abstinence Campaigns*, "uses sex to sell abstinence" and further sets couples up for divorce, marital dissatisfaction, and uses secular forms for religious ends. But I don't think I ruined them. I don't believe it's too late for any of them to be the sexual individuals they want, and were even meant to be.

God loves sex. He made it good. He made people, too, and we are good a lot of the time. I don't think it's ever a bad time to have a happy, healthy sex life. I plan on having one, by God's grace. Whether that will be in a marriage, or a deeply committed relationship, I couldn't tell you. One thing I know: next time, it will be good. I won't let shame taint such a precious gift.

# 3

# defining myself, for myself

## felecia commodore

Growing up, there was a placard that hung on a wall in my house with a poem expressing that children learn what they live. As I grew older, I would understand that although this was true, for "church kids" like me, how this manifested was complicated. Sex and sexuality were not taboo topics in my home. One might assume this was the case considering my mother was a minister who'd later become a pastor, and my maternal family is made up of a long line of preachers, first ladies, and church musicians. Surely, a family that sings hymns before holiday dinners would be the type that skirted the conversations often considered taboo within the Church generally, and specifically, within the Black Church tradition. But this was not the case in the home where I grew up. Maybe it was because my parents, individually and as partners, had very nontraditional paths in life, paths that provided them both with a complex view and understanding of the world in which we lived. Maybe it was because my mother was a social worker who worked, at one time, with sexually abused children. Maybe it was because my parents had to discuss the complexities of sex, love, and relationships while raising three girls in a blended family under one roof. Or, maybe it was knowing that it would be unavoidable and dismissive to not acknowledge that sex happens outside the confines of marriage when I would one day see a toddler version of myself in their wedding photos. Whatever the case, our home was one where sex was discussed in a very real and practical manner. Using condoms and not engaging in high-risk sexual behavior was discussed multiple times by my freshmen year of high school. Even as a kid, I can remember discussions about and the provision of birth control as my sisters headed to college. Sex was not a taboo topic in our home. In fact, I often joke with my mother that she had to be the only parent who assumed their kids were sexually active even when they were not.

Likewise, sexuality was a topic that was also openly discussed in my home. It is often said that sexuality, specifically homosexuality, was either discussed in Christian homes as a demonic, perverse nature or a lifestyle from which persons needed "deliverance." However, I can remember being taught the humanity of LGBT persons very early in life. In fact, when I was a kid, my mother had not long gone into the ministry when she went to visit a male member of our church who was in distress. Not uncommon for most ministry kids with working parents, she took me along. There were plenty of rumors about this man's sexuality, and this murmuring was confirmed when my inquisitive child-self overheard this man confiding in my mother that his boyfriend for many years had decided to leave him. I had certainly heard the aforementioned negative attributes expressed about gay men from other "Christians." Yet, I also saw my mother comforting this man, telling him how it was okay to grieve a love lost. She told him that he would find love again and that God loved him. When we got out to the car (because as progressive as my parents may have been, I knew to stay *out of grown folks' business* while I was in that house), I asked my mom why she was so nice to the man when people said she shouldn't be. In many ways, I had been indoctrinated by the church folks of my childhood despite my parents never teaching me anything like that. I suppose that's how powerful that kind programming can be. Nevertheless, my mother's reply, the reply that undoubtedly had a lasting impact on me, was this: "Felecia, when he cried on my shoulder, he was just a person who was hurting, a person who had lost someone they loved. Who he loved doesn't really matter."

These were the lessons I was taught growing up. My parents did not shy away when it came to the topic of sex. They were frank and honest, and I am forever grateful for that because I now know it was not the norm.

Church was another story.

With all of the openness I enjoyed at home, I went to church on Sundays—Sunday School, Vacation Bible Schools, and other various church activities—where the fictive kin I called "church family" also taught me that sex before marriage was a sin. They said that girls who engaged in sexual activity before marriage were undesirable and that virginity was the gold standard of Christian single womanhood. As I shared earlier, it was there that I learned that LGBT persons were somehow deviant to the will of God. Even more specifically, I learned that there was this classification of good and bad girls. Usually the determination of who was what had to do with a girl's level of sexual activity and the types of sexual activities in which she engaged.

I wish I could say that none of this indoctrination fazed me. That my honest, accidentally progressive parents and household created a barrier against the harshness of those words and teachings. But that would not be true. Church and church culture were as much a part of my identity as being a Black woman raised below the Mason-Dixon Line. Truth is, these things are still a major part of my identity. So, though my parents never taught me to be ashamed of sex and instead taught me to be responsible and safe, and to have sexual agency and sexual intelligence, I still believed that somehow I was more valuable if I was not having sex. I began to believe that I had to keep my virginity until marriage, or if I did decide to have sex before marriage, then it needed to be with only one or two people, only men, and I for sure better plan on marrying one of them. Otherwise, I was a "hoe" and would fall out of the grace and love of God. Interestingly enough, I never heard these conversations being had with guys. They were usually only told to be particular about the types of girls with which they satisfied their "natural urges." In fact, I never heard anyone repeatedly tell men to deny their natural urges for the sake of their love for God and God's love for them. Rather, I often heard it communicated that they just needed to pick the girl appropriate for fulfilling their urges and picking the girl appropriate for marriage. Apparently, those were two different girls. Because of this rhetoric, I bought into the notion of a seemingly purposeful piety, and by the time I was in college, though my life was actually quite incongruent with this notion, my pursuit of this piety intensified.

While my parents had ensured that I knew to have regular conversations with my gynecologist about birth control and getting tested for STDs, or regularly reminded me to use protection for whatever activities I was engaging in (we never really got into details, but they also never blinked to hear I stayed at a gentleman friend's home overnight), I was still invested in this idea of being, at the very least, perceived to be a good Christian girl. In fact, as I became even more involved with church and my relationship with Christ grew, so did my investment in religiosity. The latter ultimately turned into an obsession with being "found" for marriage (I had no idea I was lost) and "receiving promises." This coincided with much of the evangelical purity boom of the '90s.

I went from buying into purposeful piety to perceived piety to a piety for promises model. I strongly believed in abstinence and separating myself from environments that would "stir up lust." Not because I honestly believed I needed to do this, but because I had begun to believe that God wouldn't bless me with the desires of my heart if I didn't. Those desires covered everything from jobs to a husband (not a boyfriend, of course, because religiosity had me focused on only marriage).

I started dating someone who constantly reminded me that I wasn't living "holy" enough (Because we want a man who "washes us in the word," right?). I stopped going to parties. I vowed to be abstinent until marriage. And I read all the books that were supposed to make me a better woman. ALL of them. *I Kissed Dating Goodbye, The Power of a Praying Woman, The Five Love Languages, The Purpose-Driven Life, Woman Thou Art Loosed*, at least two of the Michelle McKinney Hammond series, and more. I never really got into the *No More Sheets*, Juanita Bynum fan club, so I guess some of my parents' teachings were still there somewhere. Regardless, I read *all* the things.

It lasted approximately eight months.

Cyclically, I would have some kind of relapse of my new pious lifestyle and would feel immense guilt. When this would happen, I would talk it out with my other super saved friends, cry at someone's altar, and attempt to do it all over again. Repent, rinse, repeat. This went on for years.

All the while, my parents simultaneously celebrated my heightened involvement with church and encouraged me to responsibly enjoy my single life. In fact, I remember being low-key offended when my pastoring mother called me around 1 a.m. and wanted to make sure she wasn't interrupting any time I was having with "company." In retrospect, I imagine my parents thought I was either the best liar in the world or a religious nut. Nevertheless, I am thankful for the foundation of a progressive understanding of my faith, sex, and sexuality that my parents laid for me, whether purposefully or accidentally. I firmly believe that no matter how much a thing changes or evolves, there always remains a lingering of its foundation, for better or for worse. In my case, it was for the better.

During one of these cycles of reality, repent, rinse, and repeat, I remember talking with a friend who asked me how I felt about my most recent "relapse." My response was that I didn't feel anything. I was a bit unnerved by what had occurred more so because of the history between the person and myself, but I didn't feel upset. This lack of guilt was a new experience for me. I was so used to feeling it and using it to propel me to go through the ritualistic cleansing that I had begun to believe was necessary to reach the desirable "good church girl" status again.

*What was different this time?*

At first, I began to wonder if I had a reprobate mind ('cause I am a real church girl). My conclusion was no, I did not. When I considered my relapse, conversations I'd had with my parents ran through my mind. As I went through the checklist of things I was taught to help me decide if I had made a healthy or unhealthy decision, I realized that I didn't feel any guilt because, at the core of who I was, I didn't feel that what I did was wrong. This, of course, prompted more self-investigation.

Eventually, the more I thought about it, the more I realized that a lot of this guilt and piety dance I had been doing was not for me; it was for others. I never really believed any of that stuff but had learned very early that there was a place for progressive Christian practice and, often, it wasn't in the company of "church folks." I am not saying my parents ever denied their views on faith, sex, and sexuality. But they didn't willingly proclaim things from the mountaintop unless pushed, prodded, or it was deemed necessary. Somehow, I believe I interpreted this as meaning that if you lived these beliefs in public, then you were either demonized or ostracized by church folks. And once you mixed up the need for a sense of belonging, the development of one's identity, and a desire for partnership with faith and church culture, what you actually believe and what beliefs you perform for the sake of not being seen as odd, undesirable, or even worse, sinful, can get messy and confusing. So I took the time to evaluate my faith, the Bible, my beliefs, and yes, even my religion. I found that there was a freedom in being okay with the things I believed even if they didn't fit in with the religiosity I had adopted. That fitting in is what I thought I needed to do in order to be a good Christian and a good church girl. The reality was that my life was no more or less blessed because of the piety performances in which I was engaging.

Remember that guy I was dating who felt I needed to be more holy? Turns out he had a whole harem of "unholy" girls he found no issue taking company with while criticizing my sanctification and spiritual maturity. I had no fewer job opportunities or chances to advance my education or career when I was out here engaging in the church girl Olympics than when I decided to retire my lap scarves and throw away my ever-growing women's conference save-the-date cards. Okay, I actually didn't get rid of my lap scarves, but I am trying to make a point here. My prospects in men got no better and no worse. And my opportunities to minister as well as have an effective ministry also did not change. I realized that it was my actual relationship with Christ, my belief about God's love for me and my body, how I lived out my faith and theology, and yes, even my sexuality, that was important. I had to understand and make decisions about how I engaged with my sexuality for myself and no one else. Likewise, it also wasn't my place to be judge and jury on whether or not someone is a "good Christian" based on *their* sexuality or sexual activity.

I destroyed the "good church girl" and "hoe" dichotomy that I had built so much of my life on. To be honest, it is still an everyday work in progress. Indoctrination is real.

I also don't want to be misunderstood. The time in my life when I became a super-saved church girl was not all bad. I did develop a deeper relationship with Christ and my faith. I made lifelong covenant friends who I know can get a prayer through. I tapped into my purpose and gifts and found churches that cultivated and nurtured them. Some of those books I mentioned before were life-changing and undoubtedly aided in shaping the woman that I am today. I was forced to wrestle with not just what I did but why I did what I did. That time was not all bad. There is something incredibly valuable about the process of growing your faith and engaging in spiritual discipline. But in doing all of those things, I got so swept up in the performance of it all that I forgot where me and my beliefs about my body and sexuality began and how the messages of the environment I was in and what it said I should be were in conflict with that. What did I believe God said about me, my body, and my sexuality? That was really the question. Not, "What did other people tell me I should believe?" or worse, "What did other people tell me I needed to profess and perform to be deemed valuable even when they didn't authentically subscribe to those beliefs themselves or have any actual theologically sound teachings with which to back it up?"

The questions were clear. Could I decipher what was God and what was patriarchy? Could I figure out what was healthy spiritual discipline and what was the perpetuating of politics of respectability and the desire to outrun White society's Black women tropes cloaked in a luring disguise of theology and the faith of our fathers and mothers? Who did I say Christ was? What was the life I believed God wanted me to live? Did God want me to be a "good church girl" or did She want me to be a reflection of Her? These were the questions I wrestled with in order to achieve a happy, balanced, and healthy understanding of not only myself but also my sexuality. No one could make those decisions for me. I had to make them myself. And I had all the intelligence, information, and spiritual capacity and connection to do so.

And maybe that is what my parents actually wanted me to understand all along. I joked before that my parents, though very churchy, were also accidentally progressive Christians when it came to areas of gender, sex, and sexuality. But, in actuality, I think they just wanted to make sure that their kids had all the information to make the best decisions for themselves. Not just when it came to where to go to school, how to pick a career, and how to make friends, but also when it came to forming our spiritual and sexual identities. They didn't present one side of the story only for us to go out of the front door and not understand the world, people, and how our bodies, thoughts, and feelings interacted with that world and those people. They built our family on a strong Christian foundation. But they also reiterated that a dogma that did not acknowledge humanity was dangerous. They taught us about sexual health and making healthy sexual choices. They taught us abstinence, but they also taught us about condoms, birth control, and various sexual identities. They encouraged and celebrated marriage. But they also stressed that marriage isn't for everyone, and there are all kinds of ways to be partnered. They celebrated parenthood but also reminded us that our worth as women wasn't wrapped up in our ovaries. They didn't tell us what decisions to make. They taught us how to make wise decisions. They also taught us the power of God's grace when those decisions didn't always pan out the way we hoped or the consequences weren't what we expected. They taught us that God loved us without condition. He loved the parts of us that laid prostrate in intense worship. She loved parts of us that laid in beds of passion with those with whom we found a physical connection. Even if the latter was on a honeymoon night or after a night of deep connection with another soul. God loves us. More specifically, God loves me. God loves all of me. The great, the not-so-great, the chaste, and the not-so-chaste.

 As I continue along my Christian journey, I am learning how to embrace the complexities of my faith walk, particularly as it pertains to my sexual identity. I am not saying that I think you are bound or backward if you subscribe to abstinence. Nor am I saying the only marker of a liberated, womanist, Christian Black woman is that you are gettin' it in every time the doors of the church or your home are open. But what I hope to convey, from my very limited understanding, during my short time here on this earth, is that these decisions should be based on your own relationship with God and not on a doctrine that wraps your value or your Christian identity within them. If God loves me in whatever state I am in, then I must believe that he loves other people, too—without condition. And if God loves me, who are church people to ascribe a value to my personhood based on the performance or perceived knowledge of my sexuality? Who am I to let them? How can I engage in such a limited understanding of my Christian identity when I have access to so much knowledge and such a large God?

God did not give us a spirit of fear, but of love and of a sound mind. So let us all continue to push against shallow definitions of Christian sexuality and the dichotomous binary of "good church girls" and Jezebels, hoes, and harlots. Let us define who we are sexually as Christians through our own relationship with God. Though the physical church and church culture can fortify us, encourage us, and even minister to us, we must be careful that the church doesn't define us. And in a world that tells us that we are defined by what and whom we are connected to— that can be a radical stance. But it can also be the first step to revelation. The Bible says to train up a child in the way they should go, and they will not depart from it. It seems my parents knew there would be many voices and signs along the way that would try to tell me who I was and what path I needed to take to fulfill other people's (and at times my own) limited definitions of me. Lucky for me, my parents taught me that no one defined me nor my Christian identity, sexuality and all, but me and God. My parents may have been accidentally progressive Christians, but they were purposefully authentic. They lived as fully human and fully Christians. And thus, a child learns what they live.

# 4

# pearls for my mother

## jessica "souletic" harris

My mother wasn't allowed to be born again. Her sexuality was placed on the altar to be scrutinized instead of offered up with prayers. Her body was seen as bad. Her sexuality disenfranchised her say. Let me explain.

While I cannot say that I grew up in the church, what I can say is, from a very early age, I've maintained a strong personal relationship with God. But I never dismissed church. This, despite the fact that I watched the Church dismiss my mother, who is the matriarch of my family and was fundamentally the head of our household. She was a young mother with five children at the time, looking for a foundation to stand on and a support system. Unfortunately, she was denied membership into the church because she was an unwed mother of five with the sixth child on the way. My mother's womanhood was on trial. The church basically told my mother that women were to submit to men, and so she should marry my stepfather if she wanted to be an active member.

Apparently, to the Reformed Baptist congregants, my mother was not *to die for* unless there was a mortal man whom she was to submit to first. And even then, her worthiness and stewardship were denied before God.

In asking for membership, fellowship, and ultimately relationship, my mother was left vulnerable and exposed. No one looked for her exposed precious soul but only at her naked body. And she wasn't allowed to be naked and unashamed. She wasn't allowed to lay her burdens down there. She wasn't even allowed to wear white on her wedding day.

But blessed are pure at heart, for they shall see God.

God shall see them.

This would soon be my very first lesson on the importance of cultivating a personal relationship with God.

There was so much opposition against my mother, but very little accountability and accusation in the direction of my stepfather. Not that an overt reprimanding from the church was necessary for two consenting adults. Moreover, condemnation is not the judgment of man but of God. However, my mother was the only one being prosecuted, and her womanhood was examined as a measure of her worthiness to God and her relationship with him. Ironically, my mother prematurely entered into a marriage with my stepfather under the pretenses that this act would solidify her access to the church.

Turns out it didn't.

Where in the world does a woman find herself? Where in the church does a woman find herself? As a young woman of God filled with both the Holy Spirit and a buffet of black girl magic, I'm still searching for space where I can fully be this powerful bold expression of God. Much like my mother, in every defining role in my life, some man is trying to make me a voiceless vagina. My ability to exist freely, whole-bodied, and circumspectly as both black and woman, as well as, ALL God and fully God's, is challenged egregiously. In this male-dominated society, I am salt and sand to both carnal and pious men.

Women are not man's vision. The woman was created while the man slept. The supervision of woman was imagined by God. Genesis 2:18 says, "And the Lord God said, it is not good that the man is alone; I will make a helpmeet for him." When God created both male and female in His image, He saw that it was very good. He saw both man and woman as very good.

"And Adam said, this is now bone of my bones and flesh of my flesh and she shall be called Woman because she was taken from Man." -Genesis 2:23

In essence, my body is good.

"Therefore shall a man leave his father and his mother and shall cleave unto his wife and they shall be one flesh. And they were both naked, the man and the woman were not ashamed." -Genesis 2:24

In essence, my sexuality is also good.

My womanhood and my beautiful blackness have been antagonized since birth and crucified daily. As a black woman and a woman of God, my virtue, value, and necessity are weighed heavy and unbalanced on a deep and empty scale of social order and moral hierarchy, one that puts the men first and only. Both men and women are univocally called to a purpose and created with a power. Yet and still, I find it difficult to stand firm as an active member of society, as well as, a substantial member of the church. In the secular world, I'm viewed as a minority, which by definition means child-like and in need of an overseer. And in the Church, which is supposed to be the body of Christ, I'm seen as the weaker member and my ability to function fully in the kingdom of God is misinterpreted, displaced, and abused by misogynist leadership.

Men are head of the house, head of state, and head of Church in our society. Women are pervasively kept silent in all those dwelling spaces and, in many cases, experiencing a paradoxical existence. This, despite the fact that women are also amazing sentient beings with the ability to be spine and soul if not head and body, at least. God said, let us make man in our image, after our likeness, and in the image of God created he him; male and female created he them (see Genesis 1:26). Both men and women were made in the image of God, and therefore, by nature, men and women are equally valued in the body of Christ. Equally given dominion. Both men and women have precedence and are stewards over what God has created. Nevertheless, in my experience, women are under fire and forced to be the limited beta with boundaries while men are boundless and dominant.

As Christians, we understand that Christ is the head of the house, state, and the church. We believe that the church is the body of Christ. There is one body with many members in which Christ is the head. However, too many of our leaders tend to forget that the Church submits to Christ. Submission and headship belong to both men and woman mutually and both are to be respected mutually. Authority is not only the domain of men.

Let me have my sexuality and my say!

"Just as a body, though one, has many parts, but all its many parts form one body, so it is with Christ. For we were all baptized by one Spirit so as to form one body—whether Jews or Gentiles, slave or free—and we were all given the one Spirit to drink. Even so the body is not made up of one part but of many." -1 Corinthians 12:12-14

Sexuality and religion go hand in hand. The body of Christ is both male and female. The body of Christ does have a vagina. That body is good, and my sexuality is biblical. It is not a predestined condition for arrested development. My sexuality is a human condition and is a source of pleasure opposed to pain. I'm called to be fruitful and multiply. I'm equally called be a mutual steward in the kingdom of God. Ownership belongs to me. I'm well equipped for purpose and revelation. I'm called to be born again and to take up my cross and walk.

I'm not a faceless, voiceless, memberless vagina. My sexuality is praised, and my body is justified and not forsaken. My body is not a fiery furnace. My soul is significant in the body of Christ. My body is not sackcloth and ashes, but it is a temple, a dwelling place for God. A dwelling place for me.

"You are the salt of the earth. But if the salt loses its saltiness, how can it be made salty again? It is no longer good for anything, except to be thrown out and trampled underfoot. You are the light of the world. A town built on a hill cannot be hidden. Neither do people light a lamp and put it under a bowl. Instead they put it on its stand, and it gives light to everyone in the house. In the same way, let your light shine before others, that they may see your good deeds and glorify your Father in heaven." - Matthew 5:13-16

The sand and salt have made me a pearl. I will not be trampled under the feet of dogmas and swine. My body is a part of the Trinity.

My mother is a pearl. She is precious in the sight of God. Turns out she is to die for. Just as she is. Just as she was. She wears her self beautifully, holy and acceptable to God. It is not what is on the outside but what is on the inside that matters to God.

"The Lord does not look at the things man looks at. A man looks at the outward appearance, but the Lord looks at the heart." -1 Samuel 16:7

My mother and I are both Mary. We are Magdelene. Should we be any woman, it is not Adam's Eve, but instead we are the women of Christ. We live not eating from a tree. We bear the tree. We have taken up our crosses and followed God. We have worn our scarlet letters and have received our burnt offerings.

Our bodies are holy and acceptable to the Lord; this is our reasonable service.

My mother is still searching for a church home. She has grown in God in spite of her adversity with the Church. She now knows home is where the heart is and that God first loved her. My mother and stepfather are still married, and they both have a personal relationship with God. God created us for relationship, called us to stewardship, and invites us to fellowship. Church is where two or three are gathered. We are all on our journeys. There is a story inside of us. It is our account. Shameless and spotless we are in the sight of God.

I have put oil in my lamp, and there have been ashes on my head. When I was naked, love clothed me. I'm currently a part of a church, and God has blessed me to teach Sunday School and minister to whomever He puts on my path. Many men have tried to bury my authority, but Glory be to God, my influence cannot be earthened. I am an unearthened vessel.

I'm not naked and still hiding from God. I am the salt and the light. The body of Christ also has a heartbeat, and love is emphasized over sexuality in the kingdom of God. Greater is He who is in me than he who is in the world. My place in the world is in the Body of Christ. I'm a powerful source of God's expression.

# 5

# open legs didn't heal my empty heart

## angela johnson ayers

I will never forget that day. It was a Wednesday night bible study, and all of a sudden, the pastor says, "One of our congregants wants to address us." A woman who sang in the choir with me hesitantly rose from her seat and slowly walked to the front of the church. She then proceeded to ask us, the congregation, to forgive her for a sin she committed.

I thought to myself, *What sin could she have possibly committed that would warrant her begging us, a group of imperfect creatures, for forgiveness?*

She continued sharing with us that she was a couple of months pregnant and was sorry for engaging in the premarital sex that brought this shame to her, her family. and us her church family.

Again, me: *What in the entire hell?!*

I was expecting her to have committed a major violation against the church as an organization. I just knew she was going to admit to stealing our tithe money or vandalizing the church van. But she had sex. Yes, pre-marital sex, but just sex. Hell, if she is repenting for that, Pastor might as well set up confessionals in front of the church organ, pulpit, and two exit doors.

After the shock wore off, I found myself deeply empathizing with her. She and I were both in our early twenties and loved the Lord. I could tell she meant this apology from the bottom of her heart and sincerely felt she needed to do this. But my empathy and sorrow for her then turned to anger. This woman did not get pregnant on her own. She did not masturbate and somehow conceive a child. She had a male sexual partner who impregnated her. Where the hell was he? Did she willingly ask for penance, or did the pastor "encourage" her to do so?

This was the first time as an adult that I experienced what could only be called spiritual abuse. In hindsight, I realized that the pastor was a control freak and used guilt in many instances to keep the mostly female flock "in line with God's word!" Anger turned to rage with the realization that I'd seen and experienced this misogynistic, woman blaming, guilt theology numerous times. The woman is stoned due to her sins and shortcomings, but the man is nowhere to be found, or his actions are swept under the rug.

While she stood in front of me, my mind went to John 8:1-11e, where the woman was caught in adultery.

*"Jesus returned to the Mount of Olives, but early the next morning he was back again at the Temple. A crowd soon gathered, and he sat down and taught them. As he was speaking, the teachers of religious law and the Pharisees brought a woman who had been caught in the act of adultery. They put her in front of the crowd.*

*'Teacher,' they said to Jesus, 'this woman was caught in the act of adultery. The law of Moses says to stone her. What do you say?'*

*They were trying to trap him into saying something they could use against him, but Jesus stooped down and wrote in the dust with his finger. They kept demanding an answer, so he stood up again and said, 'All right, but let the one who has never sinned throw the first stone!' Then he stooped down again and wrote in the dust.*

*When the accusers heard this, they slipped away one by one, beginning with the oldest, until only Jesus was left in the middle of the crowd with the woman. Then Jesus stood up again and said to the woman, 'Where are your accusers? Didn't even one of them condemn you?'*

*'No, Lord,' she said.*

*And Jesus said, 'Neither do I. Go and sin no more.'"*

You know what really amazes me and pisses me off all at the same time while reading these verses? It states that the teachers of the law, the Pharisees, brought the woman who was caught in adultery to Jesus. Last time I checked, it takes at least two people to commit adultery. Where was the man? Thank God Jesus, the original OG, brought nothing but truth to the situation. I would like to think that He knew the woman was being singled out, and that is one of the reasons he forced the crowd to face their own hypocrisy in that moment.

The only place I have spent more time, other than the bathroom, is church. When I was growing up, women, when it came to our sexuality, were treated with the "stone her" mentality from the pulpit to the pews. When I was younger, whenever I heard sermons regarding sex, it was always as a warning!

Premarital sex was taboo and seen as a quick, one-way ticket to the bowels of hell! In many instances, I felt a ton of guilt regarding my own sexual desires and lustful thoughts.

I accepted Christ when I was 9, got baptized shortly after, and started speaking in tongues at 14. During my teen years, I wore my virginity as a badge of honor. Here is how confusing what the church was teaching was: I did not have sexual intercourse until the age of 19, but I was having oral sex starting around 15. In my saved, teenaged mind, I figured as long as a man's penis was not penetrating my "flower," I was still a virgin, and God was OK...well, almost okay...with me. I'm not sure why I convinced myself that oral sex was permittable in the eyes of God, but sexual intercourse wasn't. Maybe deep down inside I knew it was considered sin but weighed it as the lesser of two evils. A great part of me wanted to please God, and the other had natural, human longings, urges, and habits that preachers every Sunday told me were unholy and could lead to an eternal burning inferno. Had I learned about the real nature of God, which is love, mercy, grace, and forgiveness, I know without a shadow of a doubt that most of the promiscuous acts I performed as a teen, as well as most of my adult life, would not have occurred to the degree they did.

In the late '70s and early '80s, the church, particularly the black church, did not expound on sexuality and all it encompassed. The fear of getting pregnant and "shamming" myself and others re-enforced the naive assumption that as long as I was not engaging in acts that could guarantee pregnancy,

I could cry, pray, shout, and "Shonda" (that's my rendition of speaking in tongues) God's forgiving embers.

I can't put all the blame solely on the preachers. Having my vagina untouched from penial penetration (not tongues or fingers, mind you) allowed me a feeling of empowerment, adventure, and "bad girl" pride. Hell, I'll just be honest, it was shear rebellion, and it felt almost as good as an orgasm. Growing up in church, all I heard was "Don't do this," "Can't do that," "God don't like such and such!" It played in my mind, conscious and, most damagingly, my heart like an over played, scratch record. Over and over and over! All it taught me was that God was a man of rules, regulations, and harsh penalties. Anytime a person, particularly a child or teen, is presented with loads of rules without reasons, rebellion sprouts up long and strong like a Palm tree.

Because I did not know in my heart the true love and nature of God, I felt unworthy of Him and believed that my desire to "sin" defined who I was in the eyes of God. The most freeing statement I ever heard was "You are not your sins!" I know hindsight is 20/20, but I wish to the high heavens that I knew that 40 years ago.

Let me keep it real: the years I spent single and sexually promiscuous, I perfected the skill of male sexual satisfaction. I know some may think, "Girl, bye, a man will tell you anything! How do you know how good you are?" And yes, you are correct. Men will lie for pleasure, but ladies, a word to the wise, anything you do continuously, you get better and better at. I am not saying I am the LeBron James or

Michael Jordan of sexual satisfaction, but I do know that those two basketball greats did not become great by just practicing their jump shot one time! For me, learning to please a man sexually and in all areas, was birthed, not from the sole desire to be a "boss" in the bed, but was rooted in low self-esteem. I always had a pretty face, could slay my weaves like a champ, and "beat my face" like the grandest drag queen in Greenwich Village, NY, but my weight did not afford me the same confidence. So, whenever I found a guy who did not allow my extra girth at the time to prevent him from getting to know me, I made sure I sexed, cooked, and treated him in an unforgettable way. I wanted to feel love, even if it wasn't real love. I just wanted to be accepted and desired by a guy, even if I had to get on my knees and pleasure him, rather than get on my knees and pray to a real man, God Himself!

Today, although the church still has a long way to go in regard to teaching women about embracing our sexuality, many pastors, teachers, and preachers are teaching some awesome and insightful messages regarding this. A few years ago, I heard a powerful teaching on masturbation. Boy, could I have used that sermon when I was a pre-teen, teen, and twenty something. Since sex before marriage was beat into my brain as the ultimate sin next to blaspheming the Holy Ghost, I, like many of my peers back then, thought that masturbating would get us off the hook with God as well as satisfy the internal longings that burned like hot coals. Back then, sermons did not inform us that thoughts about sex were natural and not to despise them or try to pray them away. We had no clue that it was natural to have sexual desires and the sin was not in the thought, the sin was acting upon it. And even in that, we should have been told that if we did engage in the sin, God was faithful and just and would forgive us. His spirit could help us be strong even when our flesh was weak.

A few of the women I knew took the virgin thing to a whole other level and became "so saved" till they thought they had to downplay their physical beauty and look homely to be holy. In their naive and well-intentioned minds, if they were not attractive to men, then that would somehow decrease their internal desires for sex. They committed to no makeup, no fancy hair styles, and no form fitting clothes. This is ridiculous to me! First of all, makeup, hair, and clothes never stopped sex from happening. Secondly, doing this creates a rather sexist implication that these things are what makes someone attractive. You can be plain-faced and incredibly beautiful and therefore just as attractive to a man. None of it prevents sex.

Another major consequence of poor teaching around sex is married women who do not enjoy sex because they were taught for so long that it was something to be ashamed of. They bought the lie that sex is dirty. I'm always shocked at the number of married women who have never had an orgasm. Since very little in the church is taught about the female body anatomically and its relationship to sexual pleasure, a vast number of women do not know that clitoral stimulation is the number one way most females reach climax. The church is not having candid conversations with women about their bodies; it forbids the watching of porn and has a long list of things deemed ungodly. It's practically pushing women out into secular society for information. Too many pastors who are men spend way too much time directly or indirectly preaching that a woman is to be chaste and pure up until her wedding night and then somehow turn into some all-knowing sexual vixen who can lead her man to multiple orgasmic unconsciousness.

The church, as a collective, has done a disservice to many women. It has failed to be honest, transparent, and forgiving in regard to sex and sexuality. The pressure for women to stay virgins till marriage is unbalanced at best. We are made to feel as if any sexual cravings were from the devil. I have had the penalty and pleasure of being exposed to various denominations: Baptist, Pentecostal, Apostolic, Church of God in Christ, Catholic, AME, etc. Can't NO denomination try to cast a sex demon out a young, naive, wanting to please God female like our Apostolic/Pentecostal brothers and sisters. One Friday evening youth prayer service, after a long, hard, guilt ridden sermon was preached that would make Lucifer himself rethink his sinful nature, Pastor, no BISHOP asked if any of us teens had committed any sins and needed to be delivered. Well, DUH! You think? Heck, after a sermon like that, Jesus himself, in all His glory may take a second to contemplate his perfection. Being scared into spiritual submission, we all bombarded the pulpit as if our lives depended on it. Next thing I knew, Bishop was laying his hands on our foreheads and commanding the demons of sex, lying, deception, etc., etc., etc. to come out of us. Some of my fellow "sinning" teens were passing out on the floor as Bishop laid hands while the mothers of the church, all dressed in white, ran to lay "holy" clothes over the legs of the females that were "slain in the spirit!" The following Friday night, we same "demon filled" teens were back in the demon deliverance line like it was the Soul Train line.

I often believe that if I had been taught the truth about my sexuality, told that it is a beautiful, God given gift, rather than something to feel guilty for obtaining, maybe I would have kept myself more chaste during my single life. Not chaste out of some obligation to someone's theological perspective but out of respect for my own body. I can't say for sure that this would have been the case, but I do know that guilt and self-condemnation would have been less of a theme throughout my entire life.

To be clear: I do not blame the church or ill informed, untaught biblical teachers for me becoming sexually promiscuous. During my teens and a great part of my twenties, I received an enormous amount of rejection from boys and men. I was constantly reminded that "you have a gorgeous face, but you are too big for me!" But the one thing that never gets fatter and no man could resist was the power of the pussy! The truth is I learned to use sex as a tool and a weapon. It was a tool to feel desired and wanted and loved, even if it was pseudo-love. It was a weapon to hurt, control, and get back at all the times men used and rejected me. During my twenties, I lost a lot of weight and experienced first-hand how shallow some men were when it came to a woman's beauty. All of a sudden, with the loss of 100 pounds, men now found me worthy to be loved and wanted. Rather than embrace the new me and the new attention I was receiving, I used my new curves to trap, hurt, and play men. I wanted them to feel the hurt that so many of them had caused me. Unfortunately, I was making the wrong men pay for the mistakes of others. I was going through men like crazy. I will never tell anyone on earth the total number of men I have had sexual relations with, but let's just say, I make all four women combined on *Sex and the City* look like Amish-raised farm girls. No disrespect to Amish-raised farm girls.

My truth is, I regularly used my body as a living and breathing sexual pin cushion for men's enjoyment up until I truly learned to embrace, accept, and receive the love of God. A love that puts no stipulations on me. His only requirement is for me to open my heart and take all of him in. Funny, all those years, I was opening my legs and taking in men, when it was God who wanted me open in a new and more life-giving way. I really wish the Church had taught me that.

# 6

# the bible is not a sex manual (and other uncomfortable truths)

## alexus rhone

*In time we will harvest a new story about who we are...*
                              Bishop Desmond Tutu

I coach brave women, men, and teens how to tell true, first person narratives. Truth and vulnerability are part of my brand. It's not always easy, especially when working with people of faith. It takes a minute to work through religious platitudes, everything from "well, the Bible says..." to "Well, my pastor teaches..."

Once, when producing an all-female, multigenerational, adult-night of storytelling in Dallas, Texas, I was full-on exhausted by "Cheryl," my millennial storyteller. Cheryl's story began with great details about a woman at her church who hosted a private dinner party in her home for a group of teen girls. She fed them dinner on fine China and afterward gathered them in a parlor to share her story of how she kept herself "pure" while waiting for her husband. She ended the evening by presenting each girl a metallic-silver wrapped gift box (pre-purchased by their parents). Inside was a silver-plated ring engraved with the message "true love waits." Cheryl embraced this message, even serving as the resident evangelist in her high school, reminding girls of how precious is their virginity.

Then Cheryl goes off to college, and I suppose we can guess what happened.

She meets *the one*.

The one is so convincing in his pitch that she...well, let's just say it started on top of a bathroom sink and finished on a dirty mattress (sans frame) in his bedroom. Now I'm listening to her tell this story and loving every minute of it. So much so that I cannot wait to see how it wraps.

Then she did what I was hoping she wouldn't.

She launches into this whole "I felt so convicted" speech. As disappointed as I was that this was the direction her story went, I believed her. I also understood there were deeper truths to this story.

I asked, "How long were you two together?"

"Five years," she said.

"How often did you have sex after that first time when you felt so convicted?"

Pregnant pause.

"Uh, a lot."

"Were you convicted after each dalliance?"

"Yes."

"But you kept doing it."

"Yes."

"Why?"

She thought about it for a bit, and finally answered, "Because I loved him and loved being close to him."

The truth finally emerges.

*"For the Bible tells me so"* meets *"Lord, forgive me for the sins I enjoy!"*

This is the truth that gets lost in the cry "sola Scriptura" (or, "only the Scriptures") — the truth of our experiences.

Rarely do I argue with people about the role of the Bible in ordering our personal lives and global society. I personally begin every day in the scriptures. I am unapologetically located, a devout believer in God as particularized in the person of Jesus Christ. I embrace mystery and recognize that sometimes the answer with the most integrity is "I don't know." In short, believing makes my life better. Because I believe *and* can say "I don't know" without the slightest hint of shame, I'm free to read scriptures with a reverent *What tha what?!*

As a collection of narratives, historical prophecies, poetry, and letters to a particular people for a particular time about a particular God, I'm all in. But the Bible as a sex manual? Uh, well, I don't know. If the current western context of a biblical sexual ethic includes one man and one woman, "'til death do us part," using that filter, what lessons about sex does the church girl pull from the following biblical narratives?

## Genesis 16

**LESSON #1 - A cord with three strands is...easily tangled.**

In Genesis 16, Sarai brought Hagar into her house. Hagar's role was to help out. From the beginning, there were power differentials at play, mostly social. Sarai had a need and the means to fulfill that need. Hagar had skills and was willing to bring them into the household of Sarai and Abram. One day, Sarai makes Hagar an offer: "Marry my husband." (Please note: nothing in my sanctified imagination renders this decision anything *other* than "messy.") Now, it's hard to say whether Hagar was interested in being part of Sarai and Abram's quagmire, or if she felt trapped and unable to say no like so many vulnerable women in societies where they are/feel powerless. We don't know where Hagar lands on this spectrum, but the text says she goes along with the plan. She marries Abram, has sex with him, and gets pregnant with his first child. From here, the scriptures record what Anne Lamott describes as "life on life's terms." Jealousy, discord, and power plays ensue. Unable to wield control over her desperate situation, Hagar runs away. It is here she meets the angel of the Lord, who gives her a prophetic word. "Don't worry, you'll have a legacy, too."

What happens after this? A lot. Maybe a bit too much. What can we learn about sex from the story of this husband and his two wives? Uh, it's complicated. But what we *do* learn about God is one of God's names—El Roi. In the desert, grieving her condition and lot in life, God meets Hagar, and she describes their encounter this way, "You are the strong One who sees me."

Indeed.

**Genesis 20**

**LESSON #2 - "Me" primarily + "You" eventually = the story of patriarchy**

As Abraham followed God, Sarah followed Abraham. Early on in their journey together, they devised a plan to keep Abraham safe (the assumption being Abraham's safety was intertwined with Sarah's; still, his safety first—don't miss that). In this plan, Sarah would have to prove she was a "rider" and accept all associated risks in "riding along" with Abraham. In Genesis 20, they're in the Philistine city of Gerar where, as king, Abimelech inquires about Sarah's availability. He was a leader, accustomed to having his way (and probably as many women as he desired) and wanted to know if Sarah was on tap. Her husband said yes, and Sarah agreed, both of them claiming to be siblings. But in Abimelech's bedroom that first night, God showed up in his dream and told him he and his whole kingdom were about to be handled.

"Y'all gon' see Me in the morning. Watch."

Abimelech was petrified! The next morning, he called together his council, and they confronted Abraham.

"Why'd you lie? We're in trouble with God because of you!"

Then Abraham confessed his fear, they settled their issues, and Abraham and Sarah lived peaceably in the land.

What lesson can we learn about sex from this story? Uh, I suppose it's layered. But we *did* learn that God's reach is wide and long. In this story, we see God proclaiming to a young wife, "I got you, even when he doesn't."

Yes!

**Book of Esther**

**LESSON #3 - Self-Pride vs. Sexual Prowess**

I've read the book of Esther numerous times. Definitely heard it preached, usually with ministers landing strong on the part where Mordecai tells Esther, "For you were born for such a time as this!" In other words, God has a plan and a purpose for your life. And I believe that. The thing is, the book of Esther never mentions God. Not once. But, *oh* the characters in this story?! Like my grandma used to say, "Humph, *do* Jesus."

I reread this story a few months ago in one sitting. At the last sentence, I closed my Bible and said aloud, "What the hell?" I grabbed my laptop and poured out all my conflicted feelings as a woman who'd been taught to see Esther as the prototype for strength and wisdom. I don't knock her shrewd maneuvers. She was pulled into one situation because of her beauty/sexual purity and the other because she had access to the king. What if all she wanted to do was go to school and live in community with her Israelite family and friends? But, hey, that's the legacy of women, right? No matter the genesis of our circumstances, we get things done, by any means necessary. So I laud her social and political acumen, much like the props I give to Rahab, the prostitute and ancestral matriarch of Jesus (and a Hebrews 11 Faith Hall of Famer).

As a minister and emerging elder in my community, I am compelled to warn young women growing up in church to be critical consumers of Esther's story. Church folks have difficulty with a perceived irreverent lens for reading scripture. They mesh the inerrancy of scripture with inerrancy of biblical interpretation. Truth is, throughout history, ministers and theologians have interpreted scripture inaccurately. Just because they're loud doesn't mean they're not wrong. According to the gifts of my insight, I see really bad trends in the book of Esther.

The story opens with a rich king flaunting his wealth, throwing a big celebration to honor it, giving the whole kingdom access to the party. His name was King Ahasuerus, and at the beginning of this story, we learn he has a beautiful wife, Queen Vashti. But one day, while getting drunk with his friends, he called for Queen Vashti to come and parade around for them in her crown. She said no. It was a dumb request. A queen, full of wisdom and intellect, reduced to walking around as a beautiful object for the pleasure of a bunch of drunk men? Uh, no. Anyway, King Ahasuerus becomes angry (and embarrassed). His friends counsel him on how to handle this situation—their chief fear being other women rising up against their husbands' dumb requests. I imagine them saying, "What if women realize they, too, have a voice and can tell a man 'no'? What kind of world would men be left with?" A woman with a voice can only lead to disrespect and discord, they insisted. The king decides to trade up.

"Find me a new queen."

His peeps go through the kingdom and round up all the pretty, young virgins. These women are given beauty treatments that lasted a full year. A. Full. Year. At the completion of their queenly internships, each girl was taken in to spend one night with the king. At the end of their 24-hour romp, they were moved to the king's harem, never again to be touched by the king or any other man. Then came Esther's turn. Next thing we know, she's being crowned queen. I guess she won the sex competition? The king has what he believes rich, powerful men are entitled to: a beautiful, young, compliant wife who can sex him properly.

*Wait one minute now.*

As a minister, one of my biggest fears is young women in the church reading this story and believing their time is wasted in acquiring wisdom, whether through academics or insight. I don't want them reading this story and believing that their time is better invested in their looks, their silence, and taking care of a man in the bedroom. Yeah, no.

The story of Esther is the history of a particular people's annual celebration, the festival of Purim. In that sense, I confess I'm out of my lane. As a follower of Jesus Christ and member of the holy Catholic church, however, where we subscribe to every section of the scriptures—from Genesis to maps—as the revelation of the sovereign God, I offer a loving, but firm warning to readers of Esther: tread carefully. (Even in the second part of the story where the Jews were spared genocide, they didn't return the favor. With power and privilege now in their hands, they racked up a serious body count. But that's a different conversation.)

Although I've only examined stories from the Old Testament here, the troubling narratives of sex and women continues into the New Testament. Take the story about the woman caught in adultery. What if that story is less about sin and more about religious people's fascination with other folks' sex lives, specifically women's sexuality? If they were genuinely concerned about God's judgment for sin and keeping the law, they would've brought both of them—the man and the woman—to Jesus. But they only brought the woman. Maybe the lesson is this: mind your own sin! Jesus went hard in his teachings on our collective responsibility to our neighbor: "Love them, show up for them."

In the end, I do not vote for the Bible as a guide for a sexual ethic that transcends time and place. In fact, I believe biblical narratives often check the "it's complicated" box. The Bible, however, does offer assurance of God's concern for abusive, unchecked power and rampant injustice. To that end, the scriptures are clearer: God's not playing with us. For many women of faith who feel the weight of powerlessness sustained by their silence, the scriptures remind us we're endowed with an innate ability to be tactical. We know how to work around chaos. And that is the hope I offered "Cheryl," my millennial storyteller—the assurance she could thrive and be loved by God despite the mental chaos of reconciling a sexual ethic prescribed in scripture and the truth of her experiences. She's not the first church girl to enjoy intimacy with a man she loved before marriage. She eventually developed a beautiful story that acknowledged how the well-meaning woman who hosted the dinner party only gave half the story. And it's not because her aim was to deceive the girls. The problem was her method: she esteemed scripture above and to the exclusion of other frames for knowing, doing, and living as sexual beings. As Cheryl looks back on her journey, if she were to convene a group of high school girls in her home, she says she'd tell them everything—what the Bible says and what it left out about sex and the church girl. Sex on a dirty mattress with a man she loved did not change God's mind about her. The last word Jesus gave all of us before his ascension to heaven is this: "I am with you. Always." And as one of my Old Testament professors said to me, "That's not a little thing."

Indeed.

That's everything.

I see you.

I'm with you.

Selah.

# 7

# body versus...

## leah williams-tate

I know my mom gets in the shower by 7:45 a.m. so she can be out the door for work by 8:30. She's been showering the same time all my life. I have 15 minutes to hurry up and get out the door for school before she catches me. I pull my belt as tight as possible with my shirt tucked so nobody can tell how huge it is. I crept down the steps so she would not hear me, and then as soon as I stepped by, she peeked her head out.

"Pull ya damn shirt down, Leah. And you better put on your long brown coat today."

"Mom, that coat is ugly!" I cried up the steps.

"Girl, that coat is long enough and keeps you warm. You want to be cold?"

"No but why do you always have to buy me long dress coats?"

"I DON'T GOTTA BUY YOU SHIT!"

I gave in.

"Fine, I'll wear the coat."

"And pull that damn shirt out. Loosen up that belt," she said, closing the bathroom

door.

Of course, she caught me. I stormed out the house, pulling my long XL men's French Toast uniform shirt out of my pants.

I hated that coat. The kids called me a tootsie roll at school, even though their jackets

were so paper thin they had to wear hoodies with them. I was warm with just my coat. I always asked myself, "What does she see that I don't? What am I missing?"

I was confused. My mom had me wearing extra-large clothes, and she knew I wasn't those sizes. *Patience*, I'd say to myself. *She can't dress me forever.* I think I just wanted an answer mostly. I was a kid. I wanted to fit in with the other kids and wear what they wore. But she never even allowed me to try on those clothes ever. She made me different from everybody. I assumed that she was right. That I was different. But I never knew in what way. Instead of her telling me, she hid me.

Hip hop artist, Drake, once said, "I wasn't hiding my kid from the world, I was hiding the world from my kid." Everyone called him out on that, even me. It was all fun and games until I put myself in a position to really understand what he meant.

My family attended a very popular Philly megachurch during my childhood. We attended services every Sunday, even if we had to walk to get there. I remember that time as being when my family was the happiest. We were healthy and stable. But then our household began to expand due to my sister having babies at a young age, and my mom wasn't herself anymore. Church started becoming an option for my family, to the point when we just stopped going. I'd later learn that it was the women wearing big beautiful hats, nice pants or skirt sets, shoes, and matching accessories who were the reason my mom wasn't interested in attending. Maybe it was the idea of living up to what she perceived to be an unreachable standard? Whatever it was, she felt that she did not want to be in a place where her personal business would become visible for outsiders to judge.

"I do not have nothing to wear. I'm fat, and all my nice clothes don't fit anymore." My mom would cry that same excuse Sunday mornings. I wondered why it mattered. I was young and just wanted to go hear the word. My mom, however, could only hear the sounds of people judging her. In addition, church was filled to capacity with men. My mother had bought the lie that the main reason a Christian woman goes to church is to get a *good ole church man* to love and protect her. Since she'd become a grandmother at a young age and fallen into a depression as a result, she figured no man would want her. So she tried to eat her depression away which, in a way, only made her feel worst. She was not only going against God, but she was also losing herself. In her mind, her only way to correct whatever she perceived was wrong with her was to go hard and strict with me. In a strange way, it was her way of saying, *I want you to dress nice, take care of yourself, find you a smart church man, and be happy.*

I guess.

***

"I just have something to get off my chest," my cousin said as she turned the car off and turned to me in the backseat. I was unsure of what was going on. Why was she upset? We'd just encountered two male strangers who were "thirsty" and clearly disrespectful to us. Apparently, she took it another way.

"I just feel as though every time we go out, niggas stare at you. You get all the attention because you have a nice body and a pretty face. Then you become real inconsiderate about everybody else's feelings."

I was shocked. "Are you blaming me because the person you were interested in was interested in me? We don't even know them. And they were calling both of us pretty bitches?! I mean, who wants to get called that?"

"That's not my point at all! My point is you can get whoever you want, and everybody else just gotta wait to be chosen."

I couldn't believe the conversation. My own blood disliked me and did not want to be around me because of something I could not control. It had to be deeper than that. What insecurities were being amplified because of the ignorance of those men?

I went home and cried to my mom, asking her for answers.

"I didn't ask to look like this!" I sobbed to her while my head laid in her lap.

My body was the reason I didn't have friends. The reason why guys didn't want to get to know me personally. The reason why I had questions spinning in my head about life. I could see the hurt in my mom's eyes. I could see the fear she had for me as I continued to name what I did to avoid all of this.

"I give her compliments, Mom! I try to boost her confidence up. Tell her that these dude ain't about nothing and that they don't really want me."

Mom paused, the pain evident in her eyes. I was learning a lesson that too many Black girls had to learn too soon.

"Leah, you just have to realize that everybody isn't like you. That's why I tell you to wear less fitting clothes and longer shirts. Because look at the problems it brings to you."

I lifted my head up and walked away from her. I always just run away from her when she starts to talk like that. I know she means well, but it's like she wants me to change myself because of the judgment of the world and what society says. I love myself. I love getting dressed. and I love showing my confidence through my appearance. But I get it. My mom is scared. She knows what the world does to brown girls who are "too" confident. She doesn't want the world to suck me in and throw me out. She doesn't want to lose me.

Being a brown girl in a society so bent on harshly judging you means that it is easy to feel lost most of the time. My mom felt lost when my sister had a baby at 14. She felt betrayed. My sister became lost when a grown man had sex with her and she had a baby. When we stopped attending church, I wanted to tell my mom to not allow the people in the church to separate her from God, from her peace. From the single thing that would make her feel less lost. However, I understood why she stopped. People always say *practice what you preach*, and even though my mom was doing just that, the outcome was not working in her favor. My mother's story wasn't uncommon though. And I had lots of questions about what I saw: Why aren't most of the black women around me married but have children? Why would the son of a deacon have sexual relations with a 14-year-old girl, and he's 23? Church, a place where we are supposed to go to begin to heal, had begun to make my mom feel even more lost. And instead of blaming the people who made her feel less than, she blamed herself. She removed herself from her God. A lot of women in my community do that. Women and their daughters go through a lot due to the men in our lives. We have a fear of them that we either ignore, like my mom did, or fight, like I try to do by being myself and wearing what I want.

"Mom, I refuse to wear 3x shirts and I barely have boobs all because I have a butt. I refuse to buy baggy cargos just because my thighs are going to have everybody staring at me."

"Then you can't cry about how life isn't fair." She was resolute.

"I can't change how I look, Mom, but you know what? Those men can keep their mouths closed. My cousin can go talk to a therapist. But what about me? What can I do?"

I just went up to my room and cried some more because it wasn't fair that no matter how I dressed and looked, I still had to deal with some type of commentary on my body.

The next morning, I got up and got dressed. It was 7:50 a.m., and my mom was in the shower as usual. I had on tights, a hoodie that stopped at my waist and some sneakers. I tried to creep pass the door because I knew how my mom felt about me and tights.

"Uh huh, I see what you got on, Leah. Don't try to escape pass me."

"I just want to be comfortable, Mom."

"Well, you need to pull ya damn shirt down. Them old men gonna be saying stuff to you because your ass is out."

"See you later, Mom. I love you."

I'd finally made my decision. My happiness comes first. Other people's thoughts about my body come last. The world might be dangerous, and maybe Mom is right, but I just want to live my best life and pray that my confidence will show more than my body does.

# 8

# warm and fuzzies

## cyndi swinton-jackson

It was the second part of my seventh-grade school year. Mrs. Caldwell was my Physical Education teacher. We spent the first four months of the school year donning our blue and white one-piece jumpsuits and learning everything from basketball to square dancing. When we came back to school in January after Christmas break, we no longer needed our jumpsuits. The second half of the course would still be spent with Mrs. Caldwell, but we would be in the classroom—studying Sex Education.

There were two huge pictures on the blackboard. Mrs. Caldwell explained that one of the pictures was the private parts of a girl, and the other was one of the private parts of a boy. She went on to explain that girls carry eggs in their ovaries, and the boys carry millions of sperm in their penises. I remember thinking, *why do the words sound like she should be whispering?* She continued to tell us that "girls have fallopian tubes, cervixes, and vaginas" while pointing them out in the picture. She proceeded to show us the "sacks" that held the sperm and slowly traced a line with her ruler to demonstrate how the sperm enters the penis and discharges through the tip. She went on to explain that as girls and boys go through puberty, their bodies would begin to change — the girl begins menstruation or her "period" at a certain age, around 11 or 12. Once she does, she would then be capable of having a baby.

We learned about sexual intercourse (another new phrase), and how the male penis enters the female vagina and releases the sperm. If one sperm travels far enough, it reaches the egg and penetrates it, then grows into a baby inside the girl. *Deep*, I thought. *So, this was sex*. I definitely understood the scientific part of it. However, what Mrs. Caldwell did not explain was why the subject of sex and reproduction made me feel weird and uncomfortable. Why did saying the word sex cause me to lower my voice and dart my eyes from side to side? Why was I overcome with a warm feeling when Mrs. Caldwell talked about the male and female body parts? Everything that I learned about sex and my body as a child was taught to me in those sex education classes. This means that basically anything past basic anatomy and physiology was learned or *mis-learned* through trial and error.

I grew up in a home where my parents believed in God but did not attend church as a weekly ritual. We were members of Friendship Baptist Church and always went on Easter Sunday, but I cannot remember going more consistently. Both my grandmothers were devout Christians who loved the Lord and attended church faithfully. They called on Him for daily assistance with everything. My father's version of being a Christian, however, was calling on Jesus when having a heated conversation. He would say "For Christ's sake!" to add emphasis when he was upset about something. I had no idea what he meant. What I did know is that we never ever talked about sex at home. In fact, neither my father nor mother ever uttered the word "sex" in my presence. As I got older and started to attend church more regularly, I still did not learn about sex. It was not a subject that was preached about—with the exception of it being something that no respectable woman enjoys. So how did I learn about sex? Osmosis, I suppose.

From the time I was a child, to becoming a young mother and wife, through getting divorced and becoming a single mom, to becoming a middle-aged-possibly-forever-alone-woman, sex has always had the same meaning. To me, it was essentially the thing that you do when you are married with the man who makes you feel warm and fuzzy inside when he looked at you. Outside of that, it was wrong and nasty. At least, that was the message that was communicated to me in church.

My first recollection of sexual attraction was the feeling. It was a warmth that was inexplainable—the kind that overtakes your senses. People think that feelings of desire begin post-puberty. I beg to differ. Do you remember your first crush? I do. His name was Ernest Bailey, and he looked like a cross between Michael Jackson and Billy Dee Williams with the biggest copper-colored afro that I had ever seen. He was wonderful. He was the first boy to make me feel the *warm and fuzzies*. He was a work of art.

I was in the first grade, six-years-old. I loved him from afar through the third grade. We moved during my third-grade year, and I had to change schools. I thought I would never see him or his copper afro again. I was wrong. One weekend, my new best friend Linda had a cookout, and I went over to her house to enjoy the company of her and her family in the backyard. I remember going into the backyard and feeling time freeze. There he was—none other than Ernest Bailey in the flesh. I was in the fourth grade, and I had not seen him in at least a year. I could not move. I just sat down and perspired silently for the rest of the afternoon. I couldn't even reach up and wipe my brow. Maybe I blacked out? I don't know. I cannot remember anything else that happened that day. All I know is I saw him, and a warmth oozed through my body that I would begin to associate with serious physical attraction. In fact, to this day, forty plus years later, it's that feeling that tells me when I am sexually attracted to someone. Since that day, I have sought that feeling with vigor—constantly hoping and praying that one day I would feel that way about someone, and they would reciprocate my feelings.

Fast forward through junior high and high school—I never had a boyfriend. I had boys "like" me, but that meant nothing because in the '80s, boys liked everybody. It also seemed that everyone I knew was having sex except for me. I'm not sure I was really all that interested in having sex. I mean, I still remembered the beauty of the warm and fuzzies; however, no one since Ernest Bailey had evoked those feelings in me.

Since I graduated from high school and went to college with no semblance of a boyfriend, imagine my surprise when the warm and fuzzies visited me at work. I was working in a clothing store during summer break from college. The store was about to close and in walked this guy. I just stared at him. He did not look like Ernest Bailey, but there was something about him that made me feel warm.

My coworker and fabulously gay friend Michael said, "Why don't you say something to him?" as he batted his eyes and smiled in the guy's direction.

I just smiled and replied, "Nah." I wasn't trying to set myself up for rejection. *Why would he even like someone like me?* More than anything, I was afraid because I got warm when I saw this dude, and I was not comfortable with the feeling.

He would end up leaving the shop without me saying one word, but he returned a few months later. Here we go again.

Michael saw him first and came to stand beside me, blushing and humming. I wondered why he was behaving this way.

"What is wrong with you?" I laughed. He in turn rolled his eyes to the right, and I followed his eyes, and there he was. Mr. Wonderful. In my head, all I could hear was "Oh sweet mystery of life, at last I've found you..." I was deathly afraid to say anything to him, and he was not saying anything to me, so nothing was said. He left again.

The third time was the charm. I was working the dressing room, and the store was about to close. No other customers were in the store. All of a sudden, the tall, dark, and handsome Mr. Wonderful came to the dressing room with two pairs of jeans. I handed him a number "2" to track how many items he took into the room. I was frozen in place but determined to get through my feelings of warmth and discomfort. He came out of the dressing room and asked me how the jeans looked on him. And as the saying goes, that was all she wrote. He was so fine, and I was smitten. I was 18 years old, and for the first time, I actually had a potential boyfriend.

This 21-year-old young man told me that he had spent some time locked up. Although he wanted it to appear that he spent time in jail, it was actually juvenile detention for trying to steal a car. In any event, he said that he prayed that when and if he got out that God would send him a virgin. He had me at *prayed*, and I thought to myself, *Here I am*. I was the answer to his prayers. So...we got married. He was my first everything. My first real kiss. My first sexual encounter. My first love. Whatever I did not learn from those sex education classes, I learned from him. The Baptist church of the early 1980s still did not teach children or young adults about sex. The only thing that we were taught was that it was wrong to do unless you were married. If anyone had sex outside of marriage, they were doomed to the fire of hell.

So now that I was married, I could have sex freely without the penalty of sin! Accordingly, I believed that sex was equal to love. No one ever told or showed me different. Mr. Wonderful and I never had an issue in the department of sex. We were completely attracted to one another in a way that was almost magnetic. Regardless of disagreements, misunderstandings, or full-blown arguments, sex was never withheld by either party. So when our relationship began to fall apart, I was completely taken aback. I thought that sex would save my marriage, but it didn't. My parents had never talked to me about this kind of thing, so I couldn't go to them. My pastor, a traditional-read-a-scripture-hoop-it-out-sweat-sip-and-sit-kind of preacher never talked about sex so I did not feel comfortable going to him and asking him anything either. I was left with what I thought was a normal relationship—but, in truth, it was only sex. There was no relationship. How could anyone feel warm and fuzzy with multiple people simultaneously when you were married? I suppose in the end we all have different understandings of the value of "the warm and fuzzies." Apparently, Mr. Wonderful had enough warm and fuzzies to spread around.

After things completely fell apart, and we separated, I remained attracted to this man who was now my ex-husband. He was, after all, my first everything. Sure, I knew that he had been unfaithful and suspected that he had been a serial cheater. He was verbally, emotionally, and physically abusive at times, but deep down, because I was never taught different, I thought that if only he could feel the warm and fuzzies with me, we would be okay. There would be a chance for us. It would work out. Often, our parents neglect to teach us the things that we need to know about sex and relationships. School does what it can to teach us what the educators believe that we should know. The Church is the community of believers that God sends to teach us all of the things that we need to know for life and relationships — or at least direct us to someone or something that can teach us. This should include sex. It often does not. Up to this particular point in my life, the church had utterly forsaken me.

Fast forward five years and three moves, and I'd begun to consider myself a re-virgin. It was the mid '90s, and the church was doing more "teaching" about sex. That's when I was taught that having sex was like inviting "the spirit" of another person to mesh with your own. I was told that it was a sin against our bodies if we did it outside of marriage. Well, I was not married, but I never lost my desire for the warm and fuzzies. After I forced myself to get over my ex-husband, I forced myself to be attracted to a new man. He was warm, kind, loved God, and…a complete and total mess. I still do not know how I got pregnant. I was fully clothed. (That is another essay for another book.) Yet, I thank God for the blessing of my son because he was truly the light in a dark time in my life. Nevertheless, I still craved the warm and fuzzies that sex brought to my being.

Bottom line, I never knew that a woman could yearn for sex and still be a good Christian girl. No one said, "You're okay. Those feelings are natural." I battled with condemnation and begged the Lord to either send me a husband or take the desire away. That was my prayer for over 20 years. In the end, God is God. He is sovereign, and He is good. He is faithful, and He is true. He has yet to send me anything close to a husband nor has he taken away my desire for the warm and fuzzies. And maybe that is just as it should be. Maybe those two things can live side by side. The church didn't teach me that though. Neither did my childhood. I am one of the ones who had to learn from life. And I am still learning at 53. I am learning that sex is personal. Sex can be sacred. Sex, for some, can also be just meaningless physical activity without love and commitment. For me though, I am not nor have I ever been interested in having sex with someone just for the sake of having sex. I think I can dream about my own warm and fuzzies and be satisfied until God sends me someone in real life. And while I am still learning, I hope and pray that I am done with the trial and error.

# 9

# taming a cockscomb

## sharon d. moore

A few years ago, my mother visited a friend who had a cockscomb plant. She fell so in love with the long, dark green, regal stems topped with an abundance of deep burgundy blooms that she brought a clipping home. My parents innocently planted the clipping within their tidy, conservative flower garden located in the front of their home. Then, they waited. Over time, it grew into long, lush greenery topped with plump, oval-shaped bonnets of color. Then the plant began to die, and the once majestic, colorful flora changed from gorgeous to hideous. Unbeknownst to us, the cockscomb had covertly sent seedlings all over the flower garden as well as the yard. By the following year, the unmanageable cockscomb popped up everywhere, completely disrupting the order of the garden as well as the yard. And so it went with me, my family, and the church.

I am the cockscomb plant.

I grew up in an uber-Christian household. Many of my earliest memories involve sitting in some church somewhere. I was more familiar with hymns than nursery rhymes, the melodic chink-chink of tambourines than the song of the ice cream truck, and the cool wood of church pews than the furniture in our home. Due to my father being a Master Chief Petty Officer in the United States Navy, we moved often, and with each new country, region, and base, we always immediately found a church where our family could worship. My parents believed in service, so they served in numerous capacities ranging from Sunday School teachers to elders and ordained ministers. They also made sure us children worked for the glory of God and the good of the ministry as soon as we were old enough to sing in the children's choir or pass out programs.

In my preteen and teenage years, the Charismatic movement was huge in Christendom. The novelty of speaking in tongues, casting out demons, and laying hands was new and exciting for the adults around me. Many of the very adults who were busy playing at being the church's Nostradamus could see everything except what we needed. Everything was wrong. We couldn't even eat Lucky Charms cereal because the word "luck" was on the box. We couldn't touch the communion table. Our music was suspect because of backward-masking, and every musical beat was critiqued just in case those drums were secretly summoning Satan. So as the adults were seeing demons in plants, claiming the Holy Spirit told them what to wear every day, and prophesying to everyone they met, many of their children were stumbling and fumbling their way through puberty and life on their own.

Our household was a musical one. This was the one area where there was a small bit of leniency. We weren't heavily immersed into the secular world, but what little bit we were allowed to enjoy sang a siren's song of promise to my very soul. The music took over, causing my little body to give into the rhythm with a mind of its own. When I was around four or five years old, we lived in military housing in Norfolk, Virginia, where we were stationed. This particular day, my mother was washing dishes while glancing out the kitchen window that faced the front of the house. She was aware that I was on the front porch with the little girl next door and heard the music from my favorite 45 spinning on my Barbie turntable. What she didn't understand was why cars began slowing and staring as they passed our home. Curious, she dried her hands and went to investigate. Mortification cannot begin to describe her reaction to seeing two, half-naked little girls slowly doing a clumsy striptease to the sound of The Fifth Dimension's "Wedding Bell Blues." We hadn't seen anyone strip before. We were slaves to the rhythm and went with the flow.

The tunes that appealed to me most were often ones that weren't appropriate for a child to sing. Jewel Aiken's song "The Birds and The Bees" was my jam as was "Where Were You Last Night" by Lord Short Shirt. In that particular song, the singer inquires, "Where were you last night, when I was sleeping? I felt a hand under my nighty creeping. I thought it was you dear, so I hold on tight, tight. Where were you last night?" Years later, using my allowance, I bought K.C. and The Sunshine Band's first album and sang "Let's Get Down Tonight" like I wanted to make a little love and do a little dance. One day, my father heard me wailing the lyrics as I executed my best disco moves. He burst into the room, snatched the album off the record player, and demanded, "What did you say? Where did you get this from?" I explained. He was furious. The album was confiscated, my butt soundly spanked, and I was forbidden to sing that song again. Of course, that instantly made "Let's Get Down Tonight" my favorite song. When my album was later returned with a warning not to play that song, I agreed with my fingers crossed behind my back. I didn't stop listening to it or singing it. I just learned to be more discreet.

In contrast, my sister's musical taste was flavored with Glenn Campbell, The Osmonds, Captain and Tennille, and The Carpenters. All very safe. All very clean. All very appropriate. My parents listened to George Beverly Shea, Johnny Mathis, Andy Williams, and Nat King Cole. Again, very calm. Very safe. Very much like the Muzak played in elevators and in the mall. My raucous, suggestive music with beats that made my burgeoning hips want to move in ways I didn't yet understand ran over theirs like a Monster Truck over a Smart car. My musical influences spoke to me about the mysteries of adults. "Cherchez La Femme" and, later, Prince's "Soft and Wet" spoke to my very soul. Each song promised maturity and caused the mental seeds of curiosity to spread beyond the borders of the family garden. The lyrics of the songs I was drawn to implanted in the soil of my subconscious ideas of womanhood that were only partly accurate. They also set the appetite for my desires.

*And the child grew. Tall. Beautiful.*

My mother had a very clinical talk about menstruation with my sister and me when we were old enough. To my ears, she sounded like Charlie Brown's teacher. I would bleed once a month, and later, once I was married, I would have a baby. Got it. Other than that, much of what happened to my body was a strange and sometimes scary mystery. My parents held a very conservative, almost puritan view of the human body. They were of the 'cover-up' school of philosophy. Whereas I had friends who could walk around the house butt-naked without anyone blinking an eye, we masked our gender indicators behind foundational garments and modest clothing. To this day, I still sleep in a bra at my parents' house in case I have to get up and move about the house. It didn't help that at church women were taught that men are visual. Therefore, we were instructed to cover ourselves so as not to tempt the men, causing them to fall. No one ever taught about men exercising discretion, discipline, or self-control. As I blossomed, all I was told was that I couldn't sit on my father's lap anymore and that I needed to cover myself up. It was as if the invisible wall of us versus them moved beyond the church building and into our home. As the baby and a daddy's girl, I didn't truly understand why these new rules were in place. He was my father, for God's sake, not Deacon Pervy. From my point of view, I was the same Sharon that I had always been. Why was I now being treated differently as if I had done something wrong? So as my bee-stings turned into C-cups, I was left feeling like I needed to hide rather than appreciate or discuss the changes going on in me. Those changes must have been bad if they caused so much division.

When we moved to North Carolina, I was ten and boy crazy. To hear my family describe it, I was boy crazy practically from birth. The story goes: I never walked until I was over a year-old and cute twin boys came over to play one day. They got up and walked away. I got up and walked behind them like I had been doing it all my life. Some would argue I have been walking behind fine men all of my life, and if I'm honest, that's not a total lie. The decades of my 20s and 30s were surely indicators of that.

The area we moved to was where my father had grown up. I was inundated with family. Most of them I had only seen briefly during summer visits. I was excited to have cousins nearby. After moving every couple of years and suffering the pains that come from always being the new girl, I was living someplace where I was starting out with instant friends for once. Rather than boosting my self-esteem, however, it aided in the attack on it as the Sarah Baartmaan, Hottentot Venus-type body God gave me began to develop rapidly. Like the famed South African Khoikhoi woman who was disrespected and humiliated, I, too, suffered the indignity of being objectified and randomly sexually assaulted by strangers just because some men felt I looked like a sexual object. Did no one see that possibility and step in to shield and equip me, or did they assume it was a foregone conclusion—a rite of passage? I can remember using the bathroom at an older cousin's house. Her boyfriend could hear me relieving myself and loudly declared, "She pee like a grown woman!"

When I exited the bathroom, the accusing eyes that fell upon me weren't at all like the friendly ones that viewed me moments before. The perception of me had shifted and never righted itself again. About that time, this cockscomb slowly began to die.

I have to admit that I get jealous when I hear other women describe this time in their lives. They talk about how their tribe surrounded them, taught them. They reminisce on how the men and women in their lives instructed them about the pubescent male mindset and how to protect and advocate for themselves. They were taught what was appropriate and what was disrespectful. They learned about boundaries, but more importantly, they were given priceless insight into the young male psyche. They were equipped with the whys. Whys like why it isn't a good idea to wrestle around with young men. This ends in compromising positions, erections, and an opportunity for them to cop a feel. It also gives them knowledge of your body that they do not need to possess. Whys like why it isn't proper to sit on a boy's lap. Once again, this often causes an erection and invites groping. Also, why it isn't okay to be a tease and intentionally arouse a young man when you have no intention of fulfilling his desires. To do that to the young man isn't right or fair. It leaves him uncomfortable and causes him to think you like to play games. These games lead some men to wrongly believe that your no's are really yeses. It also may arouse you and cloud your judgment, causing you to do something you may regret. I was never even given detailed whys as it related to valuing my virginity. Forget empowering me with the principles of ownership of my body. I was told to remain a virgin because God said so and that's what good girls did. I thought good girls were boring. They always played it safe, and I was a natural-born risk-taker. The why is crucial for a strong-willed child like me. I never got those answers nor did I receive any other proactive conversations or education with regard to my sexuality. Instead, what I received was this:

Mom: "When you dance with a boy, and it feels like he has rocks in his pocket, go sit down."

Dad: "I betta not catch you out here doing [fill in the blank]."

Both Mom and Dad: "You betta not bring any babies here, or I will [fill in the blank]."

In my mom's defense, she grew up thinking that if you kissed a boy, you would get pregnant. That was a throwback from the time in which she was raised. Back then, when a child began asking 'those' questions, they were given cutesy answers like babies came from cabbage patches, and if you touched yourself, you would grow hair on the palms of your hands. The problem with those quick, awkward-moment-saving answers is the adults rarely circled back when the child was older to correct the information. More often than not, the child had to discover the truth from their peers or trial and error.

The thing I did get was criticism and punishment. I was raised by a hit-first-ask-questions-later generation. It was a fear-driven existence with swift, passionate responses to anything that even remotely resembled promiscuity. We were raised to do and say things just because that's the way we were supposed to behave. No explanation. No adjustment. No discussion. Much of the decisions made on our behalf can be summed up in one question, "What would people think/say?" We were often treated like Pavlov's dogs with love given for good behavior, and humiliation, alienation, and minimal affection given for bad behavior. There was lots of yelling but very little practical instruction. I guess we were supposed to learn by osmosis.

Because of my personality and physique, several of the adults in my world automatically labeled me as fast. I was the one who was going to give my parents problems, they said. I was bad news walking. A few tried to isolate me by going so far as to tell my best friend to distance herself from me to preserve her reputation. Through all of this, I was still a virgin. So as the charismatically-hyped adults walked around giving everything the stank eye ala Aunt Esther, I began to see through their world of craziness. The best way to convince a strong-willed child of something is to tell the honest truth. The minute we find flaws in the argument, you have lost credibility with us.

Given my boy-craziness, they probably looked at me and figured sexual entanglements were an eventuality. I have always wondered why no one bothered to step in to change whatever course they saw me on? Why didn't anyone take the time to teach me about the mental and physical changes I was experiencing so I could learn not just my body but my value? Instead, they claimed to pray for me. Translation: they talked about me. Then they stood back like paparazzi ready to capture the fatalistic moment so they could say, "Uh-huh. I told you so." When the confirming moment didn't come under their watch, many assumed they missed it and marked their suspicions as fact.

Maybe the people at church thought speaking in tongues would cut through whatever carnal spirit they felt possessed me. It could be that they assumed the hedge of protection they forever prayed over me would ward off the bad. We were told to go read our Word to keep from sinning. While I am not discounting any of that, none of these things take the place of the tangible. I needed a relationship. Not a romantic relationship. I needed an honest, caring relationship that requires an investment into me in order to change my course. Relationship creates the ground on which the prayers, etc. can work. If the basic foundation is crappy, anything placed on it is unstable and ultimately dysfunctional.

Here's the thing: much of my life, particularly growing up, I felt unprotected. Yes, my parents loved me. Yes, I had certain securities like food, shelter, opportunities, and religious instruction. What I lacked was a covering. I didn't have a safe space. I have always carried extra weight. My freshman year in high school, I was already five-foot-nine, so I was taller than a good number of my friends. As was usual, we lined up to see the school nurse once a year. She would weigh us. This was done in an open forum, so when I stepped on the scale, and it registered one hundred and sixty pounds, the class went ballistic. News of my weight spread through our high school like a wild fire in a parched forest. Within hours, the boys were calling me Herschel Walker. Although Mr. Walker was a famous football player at that time, the name was not a compliment on my shoulders. People made mooing sounds like a cow when I walked down the hallway. Pretty much anything I said or did would result in slick comments and rude jokes about my size. I went home and tearfully recalled my experiences. My parents didn't make noises about marching up to the school and giving the nurse a piece of their minds. They didn't hug me and or tell me that I was beautiful, and the other children were idiots. They didn't give me the tools to ignore the onslaught of bullying or how to cope with the humiliation of having to return to school the next day. Instead, my mother eyed my body critically as if she agreed with my classmates' assertions. My father looked at me and said, "Well, lose weight then."

Again, I do not hold this against my parents as they were a product of the time, their individual families, their life experiences, as well as the religious teachings. They loved me and wanted what was best for me. They honestly believed that conforming to what the public demanded of me — in this case to lose weight — would improve my quality of life. I am certain this spilled over from church because back then the overarching message was that we had to earn God's love. We had to jump through hoops for Him to consider blessing us. We had to walk a tightrope to get to Heaven. The tiniest of slipups would send you to the other place. This conformity message enabled a dangerous doctrine of pastoral faith wherein the congregation believes everything goes through their pastor(s). The pastor's opinion sets precedents. To them, thumbs up from the man or woman of God could affect where you spend eternity. Many go as far as to make themselves physical clones, doing everything including dressing like their church leadership to garner favor with them and, by extension, God. We the members were the great unworthy ones, always achieving but not quite making it into the Super Saint's Club of Christendom.

I think some people may have tried, to the best of their abilities, to reach me, but their vague commentary, clichés, bad theology, and old wives' tales were void of any real answers to my whys. Their flawed religiosity killed their credibility. To quote Pastor Paul Reid out of Belfast, Ireland, "No relationship can flourish in an atmosphere of disapproval." The more I was an object of suspicion, scorn, and ridicule, the more I craved what was calling to me. My family loved me but neither understood my love language nor knew how to effectively communicate with me. My seeds began to blow beyond the confines of our narrow garden, seeking nourishing soil elsewhere. The people, who could not have cared less if I lived or died, were the ones who slid into place and validated me.

Let me be clear. My parents did the best they knew to do given the hand they were played. I almost feel like God pranked them by giving them me. My straight-laced, Christian, upstanding parents had an easy time raising my older sister. She was obedient and easy to manage. She was like them. In me, they saw their worst fears. I bore the signs of the wild and loose family members that they fervently prayed for Jesus to save. My parents made it their mission to keep me away from anyone who they felt would corrupt me. They had a tight rein on my social life. Beating the 'fast' out of me wasn't out of the question.

Everyone learns differently. Telling some children not to rush to be grown or that there will be plenty of time for boys when they are older would have sufficed. To me, it sounded like the garbled nonsense coming from Charlie Brown's teacher. That is not how I learned. Children like me need the honest truth complete with the gritty details. Far too often, people fear to give that type of information, believing it will encourage rather than discourage certain behaviors. Again, that may be true for some but not me. By the time my maternal grandmother laid bare her truth to me, I was in my late twenties. The proverbial cat was already out of the bag. I only wish she had begun that conversation ten or fifteen years sooner.

I often wonder if my journey into womanhood and sexual maturity would have gone differently if my parents allowed the very people they kept me from to mentor me. I needed to hear the war stories and understand their truths. Instead, I romanticized their existences. Meanwhile, the church literally danced around the hard issues that required work and a hands-on investment into me and others like me. If they had the courage to walk in the very faith they eschewed, then they should have been able to share their stories rather than pretend they were without sin from the womb. They spoke about their pasts in general terms. The term *worldly* covered everything bad. The word sex was made synonymous with sin although babies were never in short supply. An us-versus-them mentality was always in full effect. Spoiler alert: *us* is always better than *them*. Given the pretentiousness of the people in the church, I chose to seek counsel from the *them* aka *the world*. At least the world would keep it real with me.

I entered the world at seventeen-years-old, totally unprepared for real life on so many levels. Not only did I go to college at seventeen, but I also lost my virginity. The latter wasn't even romantic. It was more like a business arrangement. It was something peers encouraged me to do, so I approached it like ticking off items on a to-do list. The beauty of the act was lost in the drudgery of completing a chore. We had no relationship. I didn't even like him in that way. He was literally the first person who asked after I made up my mind to get rid of what was left of my innocence. It was a one-off, and I never dealt with him again.

Over the years, my cockscomb grew all over, and like the literal plant, I didn't fit in any more than it's long, dark green stems with burgundy piping and hat of circular blossoms can be camouflaged on a manicured lawn. When this happened in my parent's yard, my dad swiftly snatched up, relocated, or disposed of the unwanted flora. In real life, no one snatched me out of my ignorance to plant me in wisdom. I sought answers and experience from peers whose philosophies were the result of movies, hearsay, and their own trial and error. This form of education produced mixed results until my thirties when people began to lose patience with my naiveties. On more than a handful of occasions, I heard, "You should know better than that" or "Stop wearing your heart on your sleeve" or "Why are you so gullible? You know how men are." All of that meant what exactly? I had no point of reference.

Fortunately, I did not come to the bad end that many predicted for me. In the thirty-five years since I lost my virginity, I have been celibate more years than I have been promiscuous. Currently, at fifty-two-years-young, I have been celibate for over a decade. The reason being is that finally, at forty, everything I had been told over my lifetime finally lined up. With all the puzzle pieces in place, I could finally make sense of myself, my life, and my sexuality. I have a sense of peace, understanding, as well as some disappointment for the decades I wandered aimlessly following misdirection after misdirection. Oscar Wilde once said that youth was wasted on the young. I concur because at my prime I could have been so much better had I known more about life, love, and the pursuit of happiness. This is what drives me to educate the younger generation. I refuse to allow a young person in my purview to walk alone down the road I traveled, especially in this hyper-sexual climate. They need my story. They need your story. It is an essential investment that will result in lifelong rewards. Whether they heed the lessons or not, they will at least be able to make informed decisions. I now know the stories of my ancestors as well as many others. Many abuses, indignities, and experiences I endured, they, too, endured. Whether you believe in generational curses, generational habits, or coincidence, I can only imagine how I may have lived differently had I known some of the tests, trials, and challenges that awaited me in this thing called life. No one knows what their individual journey will entail, but if they have packed properly and are armed with a solid toolbelt for every eventuality, they can meet any and anything equipped to overcome gracefully.

# 10

# left to my own vices

## rainah chambliss

Somewhere around the age of 11, I had my first intimate encounter. It started as a game of sorts and then turned into something more serious.

Well, as serious as two eleven-year-olds can get, I suppose. She told me she liked a boy and wanted to "practice" just in case anything ever happened between them. I was selected to be her test run partner. Not sure exactly what that meant, but I didn't turn down the offer. Random occasions turned into frequent flying without reservations. A touch here, a kiss there. Groping and hugging that went beyond what one would consider playful. She would always come to me, and I would be waiting for her to lay on top of me and start the 'game' all over again. This went on for a while, maybe a year or so. There were feelings. I know this because when it ended abruptly, I felt them. The loss was as real as the sadness that came upon me whenever we were around each other. Especially since I did not understand why it ended. No explanation whatsoever, just over. Then the search was on. I wanted to feel like that again. Not the post-encounter sadness, just the thrill of someone wanting me. I'd never felt wanted before. Somehow, someway, with someone, I needed to feel something. Sooner than later. I needed to feel something.

The raging hormones of adolescence were unkind to a nerd like myself who'd physically developed early. Menstrual cycles, pop star crushes, and the goofiness of a pre-teen trying to grow up too fast encompassed my world. Major changes in my life caused emotional moments that I did not understand, and I had to manage it all with a mother who seemed to miss the supportive gene. I have sisters—I am the middle child—but during those critical formative years, we were all in our own separate worlds. As a result, I got lost in books and music. I went from Judy Blume to Jackie Collins; Michael Jackson to Prince. All great for entertainment, but not so great for shaping young, impressionable minds.

Somewhere along the way, God came up at home. But God was never explained. I had no concept of a relationship with a power greater than myself. My sisters and I were what many call today unchurched. Yes, we attended events at churches and maybe even some services, but nothing on a regular basis. Mother asked me once if I believed in God. I replied "No, because I can't believe that God would make someone ugly like me." This would have been an opportunity for Mother to affirm me.

She did not.

Of course, I know now that my reasoning was one of a child who did not grow up gracefully; a girl who was awkward, smart, and a bit of a non-conformist; a girl who didn't think much of her appearance. I was not ugly. I was beautiful. But like many dark beauties, not having someone to counter those lies made them seem even more true. So instead, I soaked up all the information I could, good or bad, even if I had nowhere safe to put it.

I had no one to tell me about life for real. No God to fill my heart. My head was full, but my heart had a big void. Sure, I had my books, music, and television, but they could only take me so far. And those feelings? The ones I felt that day when that girl touched me? Still there, only stronger.

Because I was physically developing faster than other girls my age, I attracted the attention of boys old enough to be men. It was bad attention, but I needed it. Once I realized I possessed certain 'powers,' things changed. My awkwardness turned into boldness as I learned that my feelings could be pacified by lust. Not my own, but the lust of others. There was, and maybe still is, something about me that I still don't understand, but back then, I really didn't need to. The fix was all that mattered.

I was fourteen when I gave away one of the most sacred parts of myself. He was 17. I thought I liked him, but I really didn't. I liked the idea of him liking me. Once it happened, I was not impressed, but I learned very quickly others thought I was impressive. What makes a 14-year-old sexually impressive? I don't know. What I did know is that I was supposed to be mannerly, obedient, and well-spoken. Traits I would now attribute to someone godly, like the oft-talked about but misunderstood Proverbs 31 woman. Not being raised in church, I did not know a lot of church girls, but I knew enough about them to know that there were standards to be upheld and that even though Mother never told me directly, anything of a sexual nature was probably a violation of the good girl rules. In hindsight, I think what made me "impressive" was my naiveté mixed with charm. A man I met once and never gave my address to showed up at my door. Another walked about thirty blocks to follow me home like a lost puppy. I also received two marriage proposals before turning 16. Was I really that impressive or just leaving impressions? Nevertheless, a door had been opened, and I went on a destructive, sexual exploration for about a year. A trail of souls left in the dust and not one under the age of 17. Or was it the reverse? Was mine the only soul left in a trail of dust after being used by so many? Men who should have known better, men who were way too comfortable with knowingly having sex with a minor. Men who were committing statutory rape. Men who were not impressive enough to get me to stay but who definitely left their impression on me.

Some of these men thought they were in love, whatever that meant. At least that's what they told me. But, if I'm honest, I was only in it for the attention. My body became their vice, and the attention they gave me became mine.

And then I stopped.

After a year, my torrential run through bodies and hearts ended.

Not because I became self-aware and realized that my lifestyle was very high risk. I stopped because my two best friends had what I would now call an intervention and told me that I was out of control. I valued their opinion and quit cold turkey.

For about a year, I stayed "sober" and kept the overaged men at bay. It wasn't a time of deep reflection or anything like that. More like a period of distraction. I'd discovered photography. My camera became my new vice. It gave me the attention I needed. It was always by my side, ready to shoot. I'd also gotten deeper into Prince. I only listened to him and related artists. I played the radio when there was a new album on the horizon, and I trolled the record stores for any and everything I could get my hands on. I was very good at compartmentalizing. Pretending as if nothing was wrong. I loved Prince and my camera, and that was my life. No need to address the feelings that had developed so long ago. For what? How? I chose the only other option I knew. To go numb. I really didn't feel much of anything.

My home life was tense. I didn't always want to be there. When I wouldn't come straight home from school, Mother would treat this like it was a major crime. I knew what she thought. I was not only the middle child; I was the bad girl. At one point, Mother became so frustrated she finally decided that I needed God.

*Now? Now I need God?*

Sunday mornings were usually very leisurely at my grandparents' house where we lived, but not this particular one. Awakened abruptly by Mother, I was given something to wear. A skirt suit with a pair of heeled boots. Back then, I wore Chuck Taylors or black loafers, jeans, baggy sweaters, and my grandfather's old coats. I got dressed while not really understanding what was happening. Mother made sure it was known to my siblings that it was my fault they had to come along. That was to either further punish me with their annoyance or warn them against acting as unseemly as I did. Once ready, Mother marched us around to some random church in the neighborhood. I sat through the service uncomfortable and very confused. What had I done to deserve this? What was I supposed to gain? During the portion of the service when people were able to go to the altar for prayer, I was ordered to go up. Remember, we weren't church girls. We had no idea what any of it was about. In fact, the entire ritual was an exercise in futility coupled with me taking the heat from my sisters for them having to be there. And it was embarrassing. The parishioners did not know us nor we them. Having to go before the congregation and kneel for prayer made me feel like that ugly little girl once again. I did not want this attention. I wanted it to be over and the ridiculous skirt suit to be off. Service ended, but I wasn't fixed. I suppose the exorcism didn't work as planned because we returned the next week and the following. That particular week, I believe was probably the first Sunday because communion was served. We left before the sacraments were taken. When we returned for week four of my conversion therapy, the reverend made mention of people staying until after the benediction was called. Mother knew that was directed at her, and since her pride outweighed my need for salvation, the officiate received a not-so-subtle glare of disapproval while telling me and my sisters, "Let's go, girls," as she ushered us out the sanctuary. And so ended the Sunday morning religious activities.

So it was me, my camera, and Prince until the summer before my senior year of high school. I was sixteen. I was taking a college-level photography class in preparation for being the senior yearbook editor. The female half of my "intervention" duo was working at Tower Records on South Street. After class, I would shoot the subjects of my homework and then make my way to the store. I was there so much I would hang out in the employee lounge. And then, just like that, I was off the wagon. The time as a good girl was over. I tried to resist the urge, but the attention expressed by my friend's coworker sucked me in. His affection had turned my motor back on. There I was again, liking someone because they liked me. History was repeating itself like a broken record. A broken record that I didn't buy. I *never* thought much of my external self. In fact, as previously stated, I thought I was ugly. I was not into fashion, makeup, or hair. Most of the time, I wore clothes that were too big for me. One of my front teeth protrudes slightly over the other from it getting knocked out after a fall and the new tooth growing in crooked. It was never straightened because I screamed bloody murder at the dentist when they tried to give me braces. My toes point in when I walk, and all I needed was a pair of bifocals to complete the picture. To me, there was nothing interesting, flirty, or sexual about me, in any way, but there was definitely something that others saw. To this day, I maintain my ignorance about that. The complexities of the sexuality of my youth still warrant excavation. However, I will never believe that any 11, 14, or 16 year old (or any minor age) should be lusted after and cause any type of arousal for anyone.

Ever. Period.

Maybe, I'd matured a bit, but not by much. The latter part of my teenage years proved far more interesting than the former. I met my future husband at a Prince concert, graduated from high school pregnant, and then again, not too long after having my first child, had another one.

It was then that I met God. This time, for real.

Given my unchurched past, all I knew about church was what I learned from scripted television. Most of that wasn't good. So even though I was curious—nowadays, I would have been called a seeker—my skepticism was alive and well. God knew what He had to do. He had to get my attention. All of my internal longings had been appeased with lust. But God gave me love. He met me in a church pew that I'd only agreed to be in because accepting the invitation to church was the only way to get my friend to stop asking me to go. It was a literal come to Jesus moment. An encounter that filled me with so much of what I'd longed for that it scared me. Salvation, as it's often described in the church, didn't come that day. It was too much. I held back. Still a bit skeptical, but curious, I returned to that church. I kept going, listening and growing. God was watering His seed and would ultimately receive a harvest when I finally accepted Christ. I had His attention, and He had mine. And I wish I could say "the end" right now. I wish it ended with me and Jesus riding off into the proverbial sunset. What I would soon learn is that I also had the devil's attention. Since he'd been my dealer for so long, he knew what I liked. It did not take long for that broken record to be dusted off and put back on the turntable.

I could share the salacious details, but I won't on the grounds that I may incriminate myself. What I will say is that I slipped back into my old ways. And then I slipped again. Then, again. I've fallen and gotten up enough times to know that vices do have a grip, and temptation is very real. To be clear: the temptation is not always about sex. Maybe if it was, then that would be an easier thing to reconcile. It's more about the destruction that can come with uncontrolled lust. When this all started, I didn't even know about sex to want it. What I did want was the affection that any child wants from their parents. I wanted affirmation. I wanted emotional support. I wanted love. So I did things. Things that were suggested. Things that I accepted. Things that put me at risk. Things I thought would fill the void. But at the end of each episode, I only found myself more empty. There are parts, building blocks, if you will, that were missing or misplaced during my upbringing that helped mold and shape the woman I am today. I understand who I am and that with all my imperfections, I have access to the most powerful love in existence. Unconditional love. I also know I am still a work in progress. One of God's masterpieces, vices and all.

# 11

# what they didn't teach me in sunday school

## candace e. wilkins

I thought I was fine. I wasn't avoiding my trauma. After years of childhood molestation, I was perfectly okay, right? Outwardly, I was functioning normally. I had friends. I did pretty well in school. I had boyfriends throughout my adolescence and teen years. I attended church regularly. I smiled.

I told myself I wasn't like those girls in my teen therapy group. *They* were a mess. *They* blamed themselves. *They* were from horrible family situations. *They* didn't know Jesus. I didn't have those problems. I went through my court-appointed group therapy trying to help *them* more than getting the help I needed for me. Then I went back to church.

I WAS FINE.

Until I wasn't.

When I engaged in sex in my young adulthood, I never once thought that my early sexual trauma (and to be clear, I've only been able to view it as traumatic over the last few years or so) had any bearing on my sexual health. I saw myself as a good church girl. Because I was a good church girl, I knew I wasn't supposed to be having sex anyway. So I just assumed that when I didn't orgasm or enjoy sex at all that it was my divine punishment at work.

I'd say, "This is only because I'm not doing right. God is not going to let me enjoy sex until I get married."

I haven't had a lot of sexual partners and have always been a "relationship girl." But even the few one-night stands I've had and the years' long committed relationships I've been in, I could always have done without the sex component. To me, it was simply a necessary function of the relationship to make the other person happy. It was a part of the "job" that I did in order to get to the other stuff — attention, conversation, love. It never occurred to me that I was supposed to feel good. It was never about my own satisfaction. I was never taught that it should be.

Growing up in church, sex was bad. Sex was for bad girls. Not only was I not supposed to be having sex, I was certainly not supposed to enjoy sex. Except for "don't have sex," none of the other stuff was said directly. But the unspoken dogma around sex was that it was terrible and would ruin my life. When sex was mentioned, it was something to be avoided. Sex was the avenue that led to unplanned pregnancy, STDs (specifically HIV), and eventually your whole life being torn asunder. Young girls who got pregnant before marriage were talked about and ostracized. Shoot, older women who got pregnant before marriage were talked about and ostracized. Anybody who contracted an STD wasn't doing it 'God's way' and therefore reaped the consequences of their actions. Policing women's bodies to 'protect' men's sensibilities in the church was taught early through example and speech. "Cover up." "Sit in the second row, not the first." "Don't cross your legs." "Don't sway when you walk." "Where is your lap scarf?" "Your skirt is too tight." All the responsibility of avoiding 'sexiness' heaped at the women's door. Sex seemed like a lot more trouble than it was worth. So, for a while, I avoided it if I could. I only engaged in sex because I wanted my partner to be satisfied. Because truth be told, if the avoidance of sex was an important lesson taught in my youth by church, being available for the pleasure and satisfaction of men was also high on the list. Sex was never for me. If I thought I could have a loving committed relationship without it, I would have.

But interestingly enough, while all of this "sex avoidance" is taking place, I am secretly addicted to pornography. I would watch it but would never pleasure myself because, to be honest, I didn't know how. I didn't know the first thing about what to do or how to do it. I didn't even fully understand my anatomy.

They didn't teach that in Sunday school.

So I would read books about "a woman's flesh rippling" and a man "pulsating violently" but had no idea what that felt like, what it meant. I hid the books and VHS tapes away, locking them in trunks and under pillows, shoving them behind more appropriate materials. I stowed away my "passions" as I was taught they should be. And at the same time, I was making no connection between my molestation and any of the internal conflicts I was having around sex and sexuality. Everything was a secret because, again, that's what I was taught it should be.

It wasn't until I got married that I started to figure out that my relationship with sex had been warped by two different, yet similarly-focused systems. Being molested as a young girl, my body's first encounter with sex was dirty, shameful, and secretive. As a church girl, I was taught similar themes around sex with the proviso that once I got married, it would then be deemed "okay."

Except, it wasn't okay.

My thoughts surrounding sex were not okay. I was not okay. The saddest part of all of this is that my church girl upbringing only served to reinforce what my traumatized and unhealed body inherently felt — sex is bad. The church called my sickness, my response to trauma, pious. They told me that feeling the way I did about sex meant that I was brought up "right." They also told me that I'd be somebody different when I got married, that things would change.

And things did change. Only not in the way I anticipated.

Instead of my shame remaining hidden, tucked away, and swept under the proverbial rug, it was on full display. I couldn't deny that my body wasn't responding any differently now that I was married. I couldn't lie to my husband (even though I wanted to). I couldn't fake my way through it because he wouldn't let me. I'd bought the lie that I couldn't orgasm before because I was having pre-marital sex and knew better. I bought the lie that God had provided the single me some type of divine protection that would keep me from going overboard sexually. But these were lies. I was married and still didn't feel any differently 1. There was no on switch that immediately turned me into a sexpert once I said, "I do."

Now, I was angry. What about what I was taught at church? Didn't they tell me that marriage makes sex automatically good? Isn't it all supposed to work correctly now? After a rough first year sexually, my husband and I began talking/working our way through some stuff, and I started getting wise counsel from someone who'd been where I was. That's when I realized how much the double dose of sexual trauma and spiritual misinformation had impacted me. For me, God started connecting the dots between my attitude about sex, my bodily responses, and my sexual appetites or lack thereof. I became more aware of how I responded to my husband's touches, how tense I became when we'd have sex (I never even realized how tightly I clenched my body, from my head to my toes), how I mentally approached sex ("Let's get ready to make him happy, and hopefully, it's over quickly"), and how hard I had to work to remain mentally engaged during sex.

My sexual trauma created the framework of what sex was, and the Church reinforced those notions. In an alternate reality, I would have never been molested. But I also wish that in that reality, Sunday School lessons had included some real sex education. I got the lessons on forgiveness, the importance of reading my Bible, and loving my enemies. But I was also taught (whether intentional or not) a distaste for sex, a kind of aversion that only women were required to have. And when you also encounter sexual trauma in your youth, mixing that trauma with this kind of condemning atmosphere becomes dangerous. Amid trying to unburden myself of the blame for my own trauma (still a work in progress), I was armed with theological weapons that told me that I failed the test of church-girl righteousness. Not only was sex wrong, but somehow, someway, I was, too. I was dirty. I was nasty. I wasn't pure, and I deserved whatever came to me — even if that meant a life of disengaged and orgasm-free sex.

This experience in the church is not farfetched. We only have to look at the interpretations of popular Bible stories. How many times have I heard the story of David and Bathsheba (see 2 Samuel 11)? How many times have I blamed Bathsheba? How many times have I focused on Rahab (see Joshua 2) as the harlot and not also as the hero? How often have I listened to sermons about women needing to cover up to protect men's sensibilities or roving eyes? As a young woman, when I heard that, I could only hear the Bible — through the voice of preacher — telling me that I should have covered up in front of my abusers. When theologians let David off the hook for his crimes, they were telling me that abusers just couldn't help themselves and that I was "parading around in front of them." Parading. At 12.

The church must evaluate its dialogue around sex. I'm not sure that anyone ever told me that sex was godly, that it actually came from God. No one told me that sex was good and that it could only be perverted by the enemy of my soul. No one told me that my body wasn't just a playground for someone else's amusement. In fact, I didn't know that my perceptions around sex were problematic mostly because I was empowered to hide my unhealthy views behind the "good church girl" image. Dysfunction came to the costume party dressed as Holiness. But what happens when the masks are removed? I wasn't being holy so much as I was apathetic and detached. I wasn't aware that my body kept the score every time it encountered abuse and that it would take God, a renewing of my mind, patience (mine and my husband's), and loads of therapy to counteract its effects. It's been work. It will continue to be work. But it's work I'm willing to do in order to have a different kind of life. I am by no means "cured." I'm still walking out my own healing. But, at least I'm on the journey. I'm confronting myself, my past, and my theology, and I'm doing it all against the backdrop of a less tainted interpretation of scripture.

# meet the writers

**Rainah Chambliss** is an aspiring writer by night and office staff at Community College of Philadelphia by day. She holds an associate's degree in business from Community College of Philadelphia and a bachelor's degree in strategic communication from Temple University. Rainah was born and raised in Philadelphia, Pennsylvania, where she currently resides.

**Felecia Commodore** is an Assistant Professor of Higher Education in the Darden College of Education and Professional Studies at Old Dominion University in Norfolk, VA. She is the lead author of *Black Women College Students: A Guide to Success in Higher Education.* She is also the Immediate Past Young Adult Representative of the Connectional Lay Organization of the AME Church.

**Jessica Harris** is a dynamic spoken word artist and a high school teacher based in Alabama. She graduated from the College of Saint Elizabeth in 2010 earning a bachelor's degree in psychology. This native of New Jersey is a colorful soul doing her best to live authentically. She is strikingly human with a keen sense of God within.

**Angela Johnson Ayers**, a Maryland native, is the second oldest of six children. She obtained a master's degree in public administration in 1996 and a bachelor's in political science in 1993. Her vast knowledge, skills, and abilities allowed her to acquire occupations in the areas of education, politics, and the nonprofit sector. She is the author of *Helpful Hints for College Bound Students* and coauthor of the 21-day devotional for mothers titled, *Blast Off: Launching You into Motherhood*. This renaissance woman is also a playwright, certified fitness instructor, and blogger. She currently resides in North Carolina with her husband, Larry, and is enjoying raising their two daughters.

**Claudia Love Mair** lives in Lexington, KY, and holds an MFA from Spalding University. Her creative nonfiction has appeared in *Dame Magazine* and *The Louisville Review*. She is the author of *Don't You Fall Now: a Memoir* and the upcoming *Ragamuffin Diva: a Memoir in Essays*. Readers can find her on Twitter @claudialovemair.

**Sharon D. Moore** is an author, dreamer, and lover of fur-babies. The world-traveled former military brat now resides in North Carolina where she works in insurance by day and writes by night. Laughter is Sharon's love language, and she describes herself as falling "somewhere between Proverbs 31 and Madea."

**Alexus Rhone** is a writer, producer, artistic theologian, and "revolutionary artist" devoted to candidly exploring the power of story through fiction, story-slams, and page-to-stage productions. Passionately committed to "truth-telling," Lex offers a compelling voice to people looking for authenticity and transparency. With over 20 years' experience working in the private/corporate sector customizing workshops and branded events, and coaching creative and true, first-person storytellers for live events, she is a master of curating and harnessing the power of stories.

**Cyndi Swinton-Jackson** has been a closet writer for over three decades. A Christian who moonlights as an artist, dance instructor, and marriage and family therapist, this Full-Time Dreamer is excited about the opportunity to begin to share extraordinary stories with the world.

**Candace E. Wilkins** is a blogger, speaker, and licensed minister based in Philadelphia, PA. Much of her work explores how our faith journeys intersect with the real and practical issues of life. She would call herself a professional starter, who has [finally] learned the secret to buckling down and finishing what she starts.

**Leah Williams-Tate** is a student at the Community College of Philadelphia who was born and raised in the northwest region of Philadelphia. She is currently studying mass media communication and hopes to pursue a career in media writing. She loves food, photos, and her family—the latter because they have supported her dreams the most.

www.ingramcontent.com/pod-product-compliance
Lightning Source LLC
Chambersburg PA
CBHW030329080526
44584CB00012B/780